Press Here!

Press Here!

How to develop good relationships
with journalists and achieve positive
editorial publicity

Annie Gurton

An imprint of **Pearson Education**

London · New York · San Francisco · Toronto · Sydney · Tokyo · Singapore
Hong Kong · Cape Town · Madrid · Paris · Milan · Munich · Amsterdam

PEARSON EDUCATION LIMITED

Head Office:
Edinburgh Gate
Harlow CM20 2JE
Tel: +44 (0)1279 623623
Fax: +44 (0)1279 431059

London Office:
128 Long Acre
London WC2E 9AN
Tel: +44 (0)20 7447 2000
Fax: +44 (0)20 7240 5771
Website: www.business-minds.com

First published in Great Britain in 1999
This edition published 2001

© Annie Gurton 2001

The right of Annie Gurton to be identified as Author
of this Work has been asserted by her in accordance
with the Copyright, Designs and Patents Act 1988.

ISBN 0 273 65384 9

British Library Cataloguing in Publication Data
A CIP catalogue record for this book can be obtained from the British Library.

10 9 8 7 6 5 4 3 2 1

Designed by Claire Brodmann Book Designs, Lichfield, Staffs
Typeset by Pantek Arts Ltd, Maidstone, Kent.
Printed and bound in Great Britain by Biddles Ltd, Guildford & Kings Lynn

The Publishers' policy is to use paper manufactured from sustainable forests.

Acknowledgements

With thanks to:

Katie Abbotts, Nicola Alvey, Ian Armstrong, David Bennett, Rebecca Bell, Chris Bignell, Gerary Blay, Dan Bond, Bill Boyle, John Button, Adrian Chitty, Fiona Cousins, Toni Cullen, Kevin d'Arcy, Peter Gallon, Amy Firth, Ian Gatherum, Maxine Germaney, Liz Gent, The Goode Team, Samuel Hall, Miki Haines-Sangar, Derek Harris, Natalie Henshall, Charlotte Holder, Nicky Holmes, Andrea Hounsham, Richard Hughson, Ruth Hynes, Julia Jahansoozi, Martin Jones, Martyn Kinch, Chris Klopper, Peter Linton, Duncan McKean, Elaine Mercer, Richard Merrin, Greg Mills, Bill Moores, Jon Morrison, Jane Moores, Lee Nugent, Mark Pinsent, Tim Prizeman, Peter Rennison, Leigh Richards, Caroline Saint Freedman, Clare Smith, Paul Whitehead, Richenda Wood, James Wright, and special thanks to Roger White.

If you would like to make suggestions for hints and tips for dealing with the media, or you would like to change a listing entry, or add an entry to be included in the third edition of *Press Here!*, please send your comments to:

Annie Gurton

3 Old Brewery Yard, Penzance, Cornwall TR18 2SL

Email: annie@cix.co.uk

Contents

Preface   xi

Case studies   xv

1 Understanding journalists – what are they like? _{xviii}

Introduction   1

What is a journalist?   4

How journalists work   8

How journalists behave   9

Different arms of the media   12

The difference between staff and freelance journalists   14

The difference between news and features   17

Who does what in the media?   19

Frequency   21

Exploiting media coverage   21

Chapter summary   22

Case studies   23

2 Develop your media plan   26

Introduction   27

Where do you start?   28

Research   31

What hooks a journalist's attention?   33

Should you use more than one hook?   40

What is not news?   40

Media personalities   41

Media training   45

Chapter summary   48

Case studies   50

3 Your strategy   52

Introduction   53

Opportunities in the media   54

Reaching and meeting journalists   60

Competition between journalists   82

Editorial, advertising and advertorial   84

Chapter summary   92

Case studies   93

Contents

4 Develop your message   96

Introduction   97

Why have messages ready?   98

Refining your messages   99

Message development part one: the facts   100

Message development part two: the issues   106

Message development part three: anticipating journalists' questions   108

Evolve your messages   111

Cue cards and crib sheets   112

Chapter summary   113

Case studies   115

5 Making contact   118

Introduction   119

Basic guidelines   120

Who should you call?   122

How should you make contact?   125

The pitch   130

Offering exclusives   134

Gifts and freebies   135

Stunts and teasers   136

Dealing with attitude   138

Responding to features lists   138

Deadlines   140

What happens to the information or comments you provide?   142

Maintaining the long-term relationship   143

So, it's not working …   144

Chapter summary   145

Case studies   147

6 The interview   150

Introduction   151

Why do an interview?   152

Should you ever refuse an interview?   153

Preparing for an interview   155

Types of interview   158

The journalist's approach   160

Handling the interview   163

Commenting on the competition   173

Dealing with hostile questioning   175

Radio and TV interviews   176

On and off the record   181

Attribution   183

You should never   184

Chapter summary   186

Case studies   188

7 Computer-aided journalism (CAJ) 192

Introduction   193

Pushing information to journalists   196

Pulling journalists to you   205

Journalists' web sites   209

News web sites   210

Internet-based press monitoring   212

Online research   212

Chapter summary   214

Case studies   215

8 Following up 218

Introduction   219

Following up press releases   220

Following up press conferences   222

General follow-ups   223

Become a source of information   224

Competitions, offers   226

Other opportunities   226

If the journalist follows up   227

Chapter summary   228

Case studies   229

Contents

9 Damage limitation 232
Introduction 233
How it can happen 234
What to do 235
What not to do 238
Using the internet for crisis management 239
Complaining to journalists 240
Rights of reply 242
Press Complaints Commission (PCC) 242
Litigation 243
Chapter summary 244
Case studies 245

10 The role of PR professionals 248
Introduction 249
Journalists' view of PR professionals 250
In-house versus agency 252
Selecting the right agency 256
Getting the most out of your PR agency 258
Measuring PR effectiveness 260
Chapter summary 264
Case studies 266

Appendices
1 Myths and facts 268
2 PR and journalists' contacts and services 278
3 Writing and delivering press releases 286
4 Journalists' codes of practice 306
5 Agencies 316
6 Glossary of terms 326

Index 339

Preface

This new edition of *Press Here!* reflects the changes in PR and marketing techniques which have taken place in the three years since the original version of the book. The main difference is the use of electronic media and emails, and the importance of the internet to both gather and disseminate information and news.

Press Here! still reflects more than 20 years' personal experience of being a journalist, and, for a short time, a PR person – I've been at both ends of the phone. In my media training courses I see many professional managers and executives who know a lot about their product or service but very little about how to deliver that information to the press in a way that makes it most likely to be used.

The fact is that the old cliché that a picture is worth a hundred words has a crucial parallel for anyone seeking to promote their product to the press: one editorial mention is worth a hundred advertisements. The benefits of being quoted or referred to in editorial inches are almost unmeasureable. Your product or service gains an instant credibility and status that no advertisement can give it. This book is about how to achieve those column inches.

How do you promote your product, your company or yourself to the press? The short answer is relationships. Or, as the estate agents say, is 'relationships, relationships and relationships'.

You and the journalists both have a common goal and they need you as much as you need them. The journalist wants good copy and you want to promote your product. There is no reason why the two objectives can't meet. Journalists are looking for good stories, preferably with colour, flair and opinion. If you can deliver that, there is no reason why your name and product should not be up there in the headlines. While your primary objective is to promote your product, it is your personality and skill that will achieve that. Although an interview with you is a plug for your product, you and your personality are just as important.

Although many journalists spend their time seeking out news stories, many also depend enormously on stories coming to them. Indeed, many journalists depend entirely on stories arriving on their desk via press releases or through telephone calls, which they then follow up and flesh out. The idea that most of what appears in the media is the result of journalists' investigative work is false. Many journalists are waiting to hear from *you*.

The problem is that thousands of companies and individuals are also jostling competitively to make contact with journalists and be quoted or mentioned. Journalists are bombarded with calls, faxes, letters and e-mails from people wanting the same thing as you: to be mentioned or quoted in a news story or feature. And if the journalists aren't talking to you, the chances are that they will be talking to your competitors.

To be successful and rise above the crowd, you need to understand journalists, appreciate how they work and the way that they use the material they are given. Most of all, it is a mistake to think that journalists will winkle the information out of you. Much of the time, journalists are fishing around in their questions and interviews, hoping to flush out an interesting story. They are unlikely to ask you exactly the right question which will allow you to give the perfect answer that you want to see in print or hear on the radio. So, you have to develop your message in the sound-bite form journalists are looking for.

This book will give you the background information to help you understand how a journalist thinks and what they are looking for; how magazines, radio and TV stations are structured and organised so that you can deliver the right information at the right time to the right person. It also provides you with a practical methodology to extract and deliver your message.

Interview situations are also covered, where you have to seize the initiative and tell the journalist your message, while at the same time delivering the answers that the journalist is looking for. Dealing with questions from journalists so that the answers and published quotes are what *you* want to see, is a complex art. This book gives you some hints and tips for controlling the interview so that you get as much of your message across as possible, without giving the journalist an opportunity to misquote you. I've also included some fictional but realistic case studies so that you can get a real feel for what life's like for the members of the press.

Finally, we look at techniques for managing the relationship with journalists in the long term so that they continue to promote you, your product or your company. We show what you should do if you are misquoted and how to maintain your profile in the press, on radio or on TV.

Also included is directory of PR and marketing agencies which can help you to catch a journalist's eye and get your message across.

Ultimately, you have to remember that you have no control over what a journalist says or writes, or when. Journalism is not an extension of marketing, and journalists are loose cannons. If you want to be sure of what appears in a newspaper, magazine, radio or television programme, *buy advertising*.

But you can do a lot to ensure that if you do make it into editorial column inches, it is your agenda that is being quoted. I hope that this book goes a long way in helping you achieve that.

Annie Gurton
Penzance, Cornwall, 2001

Publisher's disclaimer: Please note that the mention of any companies, persons or web sites in this book does not constitute a recommendation. All information was correct at the time of going to press.

Case studies

At the end of each chapter there are two case studies, one of a PR and the other of a journalist.

Chapter 1

PAUL DAVIES, Marketing Manager with BettaProds, wants to achieve editorial for the KoolWay range of kitchenware.

SARAH MILES is an editorial assistant on *How Beautiful?*, a monthly bookstand beauty and lifestyle magazine.

Chapter 2

RITA BROWN is an in-house PR assistant with SoftMicro, an educational software house. She wants to raise awareness of the company and its products in the media.

SUZIE INGRAM is a freelance journalist specialising in women's issues and usually writes for the national broadsheets.

Chapter 3

JOHN PRICE, a PR executive in a medium-sized PR agency, manages a telecoms account, but most of the technology is way above his head. He has to get the latest products reviewed.

MICHAEL POWER is the Features Editor on a monthly trade magazine for computer system resellers.

Chapter 4

SUSANNAH MOORE is a senior PR account manager in a large multi-national PR and marketing agency. She is responsible for the pan-European media relations for a recruitment agency.

KATE BANKS is a news journalist on a national daily newspaper.

Chapter 5

EDDIE NEWMAN runs a one-man PR service for a handful of clients, all in the IT, business and retail sectors. He needs to get as much editorial coverage for them as he can.

SAM WHITE is the editor of a glossy monthly for accountants and financial directors in the UK and Europe. He has a team of ten editorial staffers and also uses six regular freelances.

Chapter 6

LUKE BLACK works with a group of six other PR professionals, sharing resources but each also working directly with their own clients. His clients are keen to meet as many journalists as possible.

DANIEL DALE is a freelance features writer working in the health and fitness press.

Chapter 7

JANE JONES is senior account director with a City PR agency, looking after the media relations of corporates and senior directors in the city.

ALICE TOMORROW is the sub-editor on a monthly yachting magazine.

Chapter 8

SALLY PETERS has just left university with a degree in Media Studies and wants to work in PR and marketing.

STEVEN PINK is a staff journalist with the *Daily Chronicle*, an internet publication aimed particularly at small and medium business managers and covering all business issues.

Chapter 9

JAN BLANK works as a PR assistant in the marketing department in a huge international organisation. She is one of five with similar job titles, but with special responsibility for monitoring journalists and developing relationships with them.

ROGER BARNES is a freelance features writer specialising in the business press and PR work.

Chapter 10

ELLEN TAYLOR is a PR specialising in the high-tech sector.

ROSHNI PATEL is a freelance journalist working part-time and living in a rural location.

1

Understanding journalists
– what are they like?

Introduction

To work effectively with journalists, you must understand:

- why they are important
- what they are aiming to achieve
- how they work
- the pressures they are under
- their agenda and objectives.

They are important because they:

- are powerful shapers of public opinion and perception
- are your conduit to your customers

- have views and opinions respected by your customers and potential customers
- are critical in helping consumers make decisions and choices
- can make or break the promotion of your product to your target market.

≪ You don't have to be a PR professional to deal successfully with the press. In fact, many journalists prefer to deal with managers and executives closest to the products, services, customers and markets. ≫

Achieving editorial coverage is not difficult – journalists are always looking for stories and you can help them.

> ≪ Your potential customers rely on journalists to be their eyes and ears and to make reliable recommendations. Your customers' decisions are influenced by journalists' opinions. ≫

✳✳ Ask Gerald Ratner whether he think journalists are important. He owned a chain of jewellery stores and made an aside at a press conference about how his products were as valuable and enduring as a sandwich. That was several years ago, but people still remember that one small comment, which was picked up and broadcast by the press. He meant it as a joke but it came across as arrogant. The press gave it enormous publicity and he is still recovering from the fallout and damage to his business. ✳✳

Not only is this an example of how influential journalists are, it also questions the claim that there is no such thing as bad publicity, or all publicity is good publicity – it ain't.

✳✳ Ask the Millennium Dome organisers whether the media played a key role in the Dome's problems. Debates still rumble over whether the Dome was really as bad as the media said it was, or whether it would have failed to achieve expectations even without the negative press. One thing is true – visitor numbers would have been better if the press had been more positive. The Dome was the target of sustained flak and the media coverage was in sharp contrast to other major attractions of 2000, such as BA's London Eye and the Tate Modern gallery. **

** There is always an alternative to editorial coverage: if you want complete control over what appears in the media, you can pay for advertising or advertorial. These are controllable, but lack the respect of editorial. ""

If you get your press activity right you will get positive editorial coverage which is far more effective and valuable than paid-for advertising.

** The oxygen of publicity can make or break a marketing effort. **

** Journalists are continually looking out for new stories, pundits to quote, opinions to use. ""

You have to make sure that the media:

- knows about your product or service
- understands what your product can do
- knows that you are willing to be used as a pundit
- has a good impression of you and your brand, company, product or service.

You can achieve this by a combination of press releases, events, personal contact and meetings.

** If they don't know that you are there to talk to them about the story, product or service and the benefits it can deliver to their reader, they won't be able to quote you or mention the company or brand. ""

✱✱ It's all about *relationships* – relationships between you and the journalists who are going to be writing and broadcasting the news and feature stories. ✱✱

What is a journalist?

Many journalists think of their role in high-minded terms. They frequently see themselves as crusading, incorruptible professionals determined to expose hypocrisy and corruption.

Their self-image may be of someone:

- nobly and fearlessly revealing truths
- outspokenly defending democracy
- telling people something that others, usually in authority, don't want widely known.

They'll claim to be dedicated professionals prepared to work long hours for little money to bring the news to their audience, lifting the stone on secret states. Others say that they are no more than rottweilers, mischief-makers determined to misquote and cause trouble.

- Can you ever trust a journalist not to misquote you, quote your off-the-record comments and asides or print the worst side of a story?
- Do they place the interests of those who require information above those who seek to conceal it?
- Are they people without scruples or regard for their subjects who will print anything to gain more readers or viewers or to further their career?
- Or do they recognise their responsibility to see and hear as much as possible and pass on accurate, unbiased reports to their audience?

✱✱ The media is a minefield that you need an ally detector and body armour to penetrate safely. ✱✱

A journalist's function is to:

- observe and report
- make judgements and pass comment
- analyse and debate issues of public concern
- inform
- educate
- entertain.

Not to write your promotional material or promote your product or services.

- Journalists work in a non-consensual way. They don't seek your approval or sanction for what they write or say.
- They are independent.

Journalists are free to print or broadcast their version of a story. That means that they will publish information which they believe to be in the public interest, regardless of whether they have your approval.

** If you are offered the power to see copy before it is printed and make changes if you want (other than to correct factual inaccuracies), you should question the value of the editorial. **

<< Editorial freedom is a basic tenet of journalism and a fundamental cornerstone of our democratic process. >>

** Journalists don't write to please the PRs. You are not their customer or client. **

Each journalist has a clear idea of their target reader or listener, as defined by their publication or programme and tracked by their editor. One of the editor's functions is to keep their media 'product' – whether print, radio, TV or internet publication – on an even keel and continually meeting the needs of their target reader or listener. That person is their customer.

<< Journalists see themselves as the Devil's Advocate operating on behalf of their reader. >>

** The journalist's ambition is to have readers look for their byline, in the knowledge that their work is accurate, entertaining and informative. **

Stereotypes can be based on fact. You can imagine:

- the powerful, ambitious editor
- the cantankerous, conniving news editor
- the seedy, shifty reporter
- an editorial office in chaos.

You are not wrong – many journalists and publications fulfil these expectations.

** There is no classic profile which all journalists and publications conform to. They are all different. **

But what they have in common is:

- a primary objective to educate, entertain and inform
- a constant search for a new story, a new angle, a fresh opinion.

Unfortunately for you, they achieve this by using:

- conflict
- controversy
- negative comment.

The trick is to anticipate the journalist's need for such conflict, controversy and negative comment. Aim to deliver **controversial and newsworthy information** which incidentally also promotes your product and publicises your brand.

✱✱ Journalists and business managers have mutual needs and need mutual understanding. Journalists are not your enemy – they are rarely setting out to destroy your career. They are frequently simply looking for a story, comment or fact that will interest their reader. **✱✱**

> **✱✱** **Journalists want to shock and surprise, interest, inform and entertain their readers while you want to promote your product. The two agendas can have common ground.** **✱✱**

Does a journalist want to know about your product or you?

No – they are looking for stories and quotes. So the trick is to give them what they want (news, facts and quotes), which includes your story.

✱✱ Journalists can write anything they want (provided it's legal) – but they need input to create the copy. **✱✱**

Journalists rely on people like you. They may surf the net, read the news, talk and gossip, but they also depend heavily on PR professionals to:

- give them stories
- pass on rumours
- offer them quotes and opinions.

From a snippet of a whisper the journalist will develop a news story idea. They may use your comments to flesh out an existing story.

The journalist will not want to know about your product unless it has some clear relevance or impact on their audience. Present the information about your product so that it satisfies the journalist's need to educate, entertain and inform that audience.

Emphasise your client's relevance and impact, or the positive business or social benefits of the product or service, so that the positive implications are obvious. But remember, the journalist may not see your story the way you do:

- they may be looking for something which you want to hide
- they may see an angle which did not occur to you.

** Everything journalists do is with their 'customer' in mind, that is, their reader, viewer or listener. **

How journalists work

Every journalist is different and they all work in different ways.

- Some like to work close to deadlines and find it almost impossible to rouse themselves unless a deadline is pressing.
- Others prefer to be well organised, writing in good time to meet deadlines so that there is no panic. They are well organised and methodical.
- Some journalists like to use small tape recorders.
- Some use reporters' notebooks.
- Some manage to report on a conversation without making notes at all.

<< If the journalist wants to use a voice-recorder, agree and then ignore the device. You'll soon forget it's there. >>

Recorders are helpful in face-to-face meetings because you can maintain eye contact with the journalist, making the interview much more like a conversation. A better, more natural flow of dialogue can be established. A recorded conversation or interview is more likely to be quoted accurately.

<< You can use a recorder too – many people do – to make sure you are not mis-quoted. >>

> ** Treat journalists like the most important customers in the world – but don't try to sell to them. **

<< The best way to generate editorial is to say something outrageous and controversial. >>

How journalists behave

If they are any good the journalist will:

- take a critical view
- be cynical
- be suspicious
- assume that they are being lied to or at least, exaggerations are being made
- take a critical view
- not take things at face value.

So a good journalist will instinctively and automatically think:

- why is this person lying to me?
- what is the true story here?
- what is the real angle?

** Don't be surprised if the journalist appears hostile and unsympathetic – they will not be doing their job if they are friendly and understanding. **

> 66 Good journalists instinctively want to look behind the story they are being told for a more controversial story, particularly if the stories they are told lack controversy or interest for the reader/viewer. Journalists are adept at turning mundane announcements into something newsworthy by looking for a controversial angle. 99

Most journalists are committed professionals with impeccably high standards of ethics and integrity. They are under constant pressure to be fair, and most of them are. Most voluntarily follow the Journalist's Code of Practice, which ensures that they are honest, thorough and have integrity.

Many PR professionals categorise journalists according to their experience and style of working. These are typical of the descriptions you might come across:

- **The Ferret or Terrier**. Experienced investigative journalists who will not give up when they think they have a whiff of a story, even if it is mainly in their imagination. They will go on and on and on, pursuing individuals, hunting down leads and continuing their line of questioning until they get what they want. Sometimes this type is accused of putting words into people's mouths or constructing the information they want in order to make the story that they are convinced is there. Give them something and they might go away, but be prepared for them to assume there is a hidden story and use great tenacity to find out what it is.

- **The Bridge Burner**. Unlike career journalists who will usually respect requests to go 'off the record' or hold a story until a later date, the Bridge Burner will do anything to get a scoop or a story ahead of the competition. They have no regard for their contacts or personal relationships, and put their career and the next front page before everything else. Don't trust with sensitive information.

- **The Fledgling**. Usually staff journalists fresh from media training schools or colleges (freelances need a few years on the staff before they work for themselves). Fledglings may have practised their skills in the classroom but have little experience of real-life interviews. Frequently they possess only limited understanding of the industry or the topics they write about. Often plunged in at the deep end, they may claim greater knowledge than they have. This type is like putty in your hands, often a blank sheet wanting information, and is consequently often the best sort to give your views to or to tell about your product. All the top editors were fledglings at one time, and many of their best contacts are those who helped them when they were starting. Nuture the fledglings, help them, and hopefully they will remember you later.

- **Wasters, Winos**. There used to be plenty of these but now they are a rarity. You still find some hacks who are good for only two hours every morning and are wasted for the rest of the afternoon after a long liquid lunch. Beware! Though they are rare they are often the best journalists around and can turn in better copy in those two hours than ordinary journalists can manage in a whole day. They often have prodigious memories, so that something mentioned in passing can be pulled out and quoted later. Don't underestimate this type – they can be poisonous, difficult, untrustworthy and have enormous prejudices, as well as years of experience. Treat with care.

- **Politicos**. All journalists have a political agenda, and it is that of their reader. Any journalist seeks to defend the interests of their target reader and though this may not be so clear on a broad-based publication, it is very obvious on high quality trade titles.

- **Specialists**. Usually journalists who have been working in a particular sector, such as the fashion or entertainment industry, IT or business, for many years and know just about all there is to know about the products, consumers and players. There is not much you can tell these journalists and they probably know more than you do. Often these are the easiest to work with because they are highly professional, provided you are not trying to hoodwink them. They will understand the implications and benefits of your product, but are also the most likely to ask piercing questions which go right to the heart of the matter. Treat with respect.

- **Seasoned Professionals**. Can be the most dangerous journalists of all because they have the stability and experience to demolish your efforts, claims or views with the best and most accurate arguments. They can make incisive, cunning interviewers and have so much experience on the subject matter that it is extremely difficult to pull the wool over their eyes or persuade them there is a story when there isn't. Treat with respect and ask their views on your product or service and marketing plan. They may know a lot more about your competitors than anyone else, so regard as a source of competitive information.

** All journalists are seeking their readers' approval. They want the readers to love their work, and come to recognise their byline. Ultimately, they want the reader to buy the publication because they write for it. There are very few who reach this status. **

Different arms of the media

** Speed, agility and responsiveness can make or break your success with the media – whichever type of journalist you are aiming at. **

The media used to be a three-legged affair:

- print
- radio
- TV.

Now there is also the internet.

All use journalists and journalists are essentially all the same regardless of which area they work in.

** All journalists are cynical and working on behalf of their readers, irrespective of whether they work for print, TV, radio or internet publications or programmes. **

	Positive	Negative
Print	Longer lead times means more time to deliver stories and reach journalists with appropriate spokespeople Images are more memorable than the spoken word Images have a longer shelf life You can have your messages in front of you if the interview is by telephone or email	Can call out of the blue and record an interview The journalist will not give you a list of questions in advance
Radio	Wide audience. Large local audiences Need a continual stream of new ideas or stories and new spokespeople You may be able to chat with the interviewer before the recording, and give them an idea of the best issues to cover, thereby steering the interview around your best topics Hate a silence, so will help spokespeople more than other media You can often find out who else the journalist is speaking to You can use a crib-sheet of message prompts	They move on quickly to the next topic and speakers
TV	Images are more memorable than the spoken word Need a continual stream of new ideas for stories and new spokespeople	Move on quickly to the next topic and speakers You can't use cue card, prompts or any other aide-memoire

	Positive	Negative
TV	You can often find out who will be on the same show	
	You know in advance what the broadcast is going to be about and you can prepare more than for radio or print.	
	The researcher will often tell you what the first question will be (to avoid a horrible silence and to get the interview going)	
Internet	Immediate contact with journalists and consumers	They move on quickly to the next topic and spokespeople
	Need a continual stream of new ideas for stories	
	You can prepare your messages off-line	

The difference between staff and freelance journalists

Why is it important to know the differences between staffers and freelances?

■ Because they have different pressures and requirements, and if you are going to be successful in getting editorial publicity, you must deliver to each.

■ You should know the information they want and need.

■ You need to know when they want it.

■ You can provide it in the way that they prefer it.

Most publications use a combination of staff and freelances.

Staff journalists

- Staffers work for one publishing house or title.

- A staff writer is likely to be a novice straight from college, university or post-graduate journalism school. It's impossible just to decide one day to become a freelance journalist and expect to earn a reasonable living straightaway, so most novice journalists start as staffers.

- Staff writers are more likely to move on after nine months or a year because of the low pay. Hopefully, they will be promoted within the same title or transferred to another, related title so that you don't lose touch and your investment in developing them is not wasted.

- Senior staff journalists such as editors and deputy editors, news and feature editors are likely to be more experienced than basic staff writers. They are likely to be individuals who prefer the regular 'safe' life of being employed rather than self-employed.

- Staffers are paid a regular salary and although they will be set a number of stories to write each issue, their income is not dependent on how many words they write.

- Staffers get holiday and sick pay.

- Staffers are more likely to be willing and able to attend press conferences, go for lunches with clients or PR contacts or go on press trips.

<< If you are talking to a staff journalist you *must* be familiar with their title and its target audience. If you are not, find out by reading the publication – you shouldn't have to ask. >>

Freelances

- Freelances work for several titles. This means that a freelance offers far better economies of scale. Many freelances are working for half a dozen titles at any one time and for up to 30 or 40 titles over a year. Any promotional activity aimed at a freelance has a chance of appearing in far more places than if directed at a staffer.

- Freelances are likely to be professional 'career' journalists. They usually build up a base of regular titles that they work for and often take on a proactive role in suggesting topics for news and features to the commissioning editors.
- Freelances depend on contacts like you for commissions and stories.
- Freelances' income is directly linked to the amount of features or news stories they have published.
- Time is money to a freelance because they are self-employed.
- Freelances are often reluctant to take trips or go for long lunches. Any trips or meeting people have to result in several stories.

** Freelances are sole traders, sometimes limited companies. They are like all small business managers – time is money, they aim for economy of scale, and one big bad debt or slow payer can really screw them. **

If you are dealing with a freelance, ask which title the piece is for. Then do your own research to find out who the target reader is. Freelances are usually willing to give you the name of the publishing house or the commissioning editor. If you are not familiar with the title, call the publishing house and ask for the media pack from the media sales team.

** If you are talking to a freelance you are potentially talking to a dozen publications at a time. A staffer might have the job title on a publication behind them, but actually freelances can get your name into a far greater range of outlets than a staffer. **

The difference between news and features

Appreciate the difference between news and feature stories in order to deliver your story with the style format and timing that news and feature writers want.

≪ News is not always about products, news is always ultimately about people. ≫

Products are only important because they involve and affect people. If you are seeking to promote a product or service, emphasise the human aspect and the benefits for the customer.

News stories:

- have a far sharper point than a feature
- have a new angle
- report on clear and impressive benefits
- report on people with controversial views and opinions
- are more likely to have a shocking or surprising headline, with some dramatic content. News headlines typically contain active verbs and dramatic, evocative short sentences ('XProduct smashes price barrier', 'Woman loses 6 stone in 3 weeks shock' or 'Fastest widget creates market turmoil', etc.). Look at any newspaper front page. You will see these sorts of headline, and they indicate the kind of story that follows – full of drama and controversy, short, sharp and snappy.

≪ Anything that someone doesn't want published is news – everything else is advertising. ≫

Features:

- are more analytical and informative but still need to have an element of controversy to be interesting

- take a 'position', find an angle or make an assumption from which they explore an issue
- headlines are typically more laid back, amusing and obtuse, and more likely to include a pun.

News journalists:

- usually have a more dynamic, immediate approach
- are dealing with material which is fast changing and high impact
- may need some background detail but rarely include analysis or comment
- prefer snappy sound-bites and rarely use long quotes
- are working to short deadlines
- will ignore overt and dull product publicity dressed as news.

News feature writers:

- are often delivering an analysis or comment piece on something in the news
- aim to be informative or to open or add to a debate
- often offer a personal view or contrary opinion
- may have slightly longer deadlines than news writers.

Feature writers:

- are more analytical
- still need the fresh news element
- treat the story in a more reflective, considered style
- use longer quotes
- use more description and background comment
- are still often working to tight deadlines but are less aggressive in their treatment
- have subject matter which is not highly time-sensitive
- often have several weeks between commission and deadline.

** If the deadline has passed, don't waste the journalist's time. **

Who does what in the media?

Look at the masthead on a magazine. See all those job titles? Who does what?

There is no standard job specification for each job title. The tasks and responsibilities of each job vary according to each publishing house, broadcast company or channel, and each publication and TV or radio programme. There are no hard-and-fast rules about who does what.

The following are commonly accepted explanations for each job specification, but in practice they may be radically different on different publications and programmes, and within different publishing houses and production companies.

Publisher of a newspaper or magazine:

- usually has a sales background
- has overall responsibility for ensuring the title makes a profit
- decides the overall size of each issue (the pagination) and the ratio of advertising and editorial (Too much editorial and the publication will not make money; too much advertising and the readers lose interest.)
- promotes and manages the marketing of the title.

Director is responsible for individual broadcast programmes, comparable to a magazine or newspaper editor.

Producer is the equivalent to the publisher in the broadcast media.

Editor (print):

- has overall day-to-day management responsibility for the content of the publication
- has legal responsibility for the content of the publication

- decides the contents
- often has too many management jobs to do much writing
- may only have time to write the Editor's Foreword
- may spend the rest of their time in meetings, dealing with staff, planning issues, etc.

Editor (broadcast) is responsible for cutting and editing the film or tape and generally putting a programme together.

Sub-editor is the print equivalent of a broadcast editor and:

- cuts and shapes copy to fit the space
- ensures that copy is in the house style
- has the power to completely rewrite copy
- may accidentally cut out something which you might consider crucial
- is responsible for headlines and captions
- ensures that all the contents are legal.

Production editor in print media usually:

- ensures that all pages are filled to meet the section deadlines
- is responsible for liaising with the media sales team
- makes sure content gets to the repro house and printer on schedule.

Art editor:

- is responsible for the visual design, graphics and brand of the publication
- commissions and sources photographs and artwork
- lays out the copy on a page.

Researchers play an important role in broadcast media. They:

- find the right people for the journalists to interview
- back up the journalist by uncovering information, finding suitable case studies, etc.

- can be overruled
- are prone to making promises they can't keep
- are the people who greet interviewees before they meet the journalist.

Frequency

All types of media – internet, print, radio and TV – have different frequencies of publication, usually dailies, weeklies or monthlies. There are also one-offs, specials, documentaries and supplements.

Why is frequency important? Because it affects the frequency and length of deadline – a crucial factor for those aiming to achieve editorial coverage.

Talk to the sub or production editor about internal deadlines, but freelances are probably working to different timescales.

> ** There is always a gap between the publication 'closing' and when it appears. Internet publications are virtually instant, but monthly magazines often have a two-week 'dead' time while the magazine is at the printers. If you want your news story to coincide with a launch, bear this gap in mind. **

Exploiting media coverage

Quotes by company managers and spokespeople or mentions of your product should be exploited for marketing purposes to a wider audience:

- Use copies of the editorial in your marketing material.
- Reviews can be reprinted in quantity to give to potential customers.
- Send copies of the editorial to your existing clients to reassure them that your product is the best.
- Circulate it among your colleagues.

✳✳ Do not fall foul of the copyright laws. You can't just cut out reviews and interviews and send them to your clients or potential clients. The copy belongs to the publication, and you need to ask permission, usually from the publisher, before using it. Some publishing houses charge for this, or provide a reprint service. ✳✳

Chapter summary

Journalists:

- can appear rude and arrogant
- know that if they are too friendly they can jeopardise their independence
- are usually creative types
- do not work for you – their customer is their reader/viewer/listener
- want information, stories, opinions and facts
- don't want their time wasted
- face different deadlines, work in different styles and have different agendas depending on whether they are news or features writers, freelances or staffers
- are free to print anything they want – they don't have your interests at heart
- are seeking the approval and satisfaction of their audience.

Case studies

Paul Davies	Marketing Manager with BettaProds, aged 42
Products	KoolWay kitchenware and a new range of non-stick frying pans.
Target sector	Science publications, home and domestic press.
Objectives	To raise awareness of company and products. To achieve maximum possible coverage.
Action	Sourced a list of journalists from last year's press activity. Telephoned them all to tell them about the product.
Result	Most calls were a waste of time. Either the journalist was no longer working on the publication, or they did not have time to talk to Paul. Of 40 calls, only one allowed him to get beyond his introduction.
Recommendations	It is no good using an out-of-date list. Paul should start by updating his list, and add information on how each journalist prefers to be contacted.
	Many journalists will prefer to be contacted by email first.
	He should also find out when is the best time time to contact the journalist – which time of day, which day of the week, which part of the month.
	He should introduce himself by outlining the benefits of the product to the journalist's reader, so that the journalist can immediately see the potential story.
	Paul should be prepared to adjust the way he angles his story. A lifestyle magazine may be unlikely to be interested in non-stick cookware, but may be looking for subjects for its 'make-over' section.

Sarah Miles	Editorial Assistant on *How Beautiful?* magazine
Description	Sarah is 21 and straight out of university. This is her first job.
Task	Routine management of the editorial office – answering telephones, opening the mail, replying to emails, and writing short news stories from press releases.
	The editor has asked Sarah to research a series on skincare products. Sarah is very busy and feels under great pressure.
Experience	The phone rings and someone called Paul Davies asks to speak to her predecessor. She curtly tells him that Sonya Trewin doesn't work there any more. She hangs up, and gets on with opening the post.
Recommendations	Sarah could give Paul here name and ask him to amend his database. She might also tell him when is the most convenient time to call, and that she prefers initial contact by email. Paul should view Sarah as a potential long-term media contact and offer to take her out to lunch. Time spent with new journalists fresh from college is usually well invested.

chapter

Develop your media plan

Introduction

Like any project, media relations requires you to work out your objectives and plan your strategy.

You must know before you start:

- what you want to say
- who you want to say it to
- when you want to say it
- when you would like to see it appear
- where you would like to see it appear
- what you will do if it doesn't appear as you'd like.

** Media coverage doesn't necessarily happen overnight. Your campaign may have to run for several weeks or months before you get the coverage you want or any coverage at all. **

<< All PR activity should be thoroughly integrated, with messaging, visuals and events implemented with all the rest in mind. >>

Where do you start?

Don't just pick up the phone or start to email any journalists.

** Build a detailed list of your target customers, the media that you want to give you editorial coverage, and a list of key journalists. **

1   Identify your target media

Relevant publications (newspapers, magazines – trade and user – radio programmes, television programmes, internet publications) according to your customers and markets.

List:

- deadlines
- frequency
- key sections
- who writes which sections
- connections between advertising and editorial
- whether there are opinion pages, letters pages, etc.

Get a media pack and features list of each from the media sales team.

Specialist sections that you should target. Publications and programmes are often divided into sections, run by particular journalists. Select those most appropriate for you, your product and company personalities, then target the journalist responsible.

These include:

- product roundups and reviews
- opinion pieces
- case studies
- contributed articles
- letters to the editor
- readers' competitions (see Chapter Three).

Specific journalists (freelance and staff) and editors. Make a list to include:

- details about the type of work each journalist does
- a record of your contact with them
- details of their preferences for hospitality
- details of their preferences for receiving press releases and other information
- a judgement about their 'friendliness'
- a judgement on their knowledge of the subject
- a record of their relevant work
- their career history (and ambitions if you learn them)
- details of their private life and interests.

** Create a database of freelance and staff journalists and update it regularly – record every conversation and meeting. **

Journalists are intolerant of PRs and marketing professionals who have not done their homework.

2 Identify your story

This is frequently the really tricky bit. Often it's right under your nose. Stories may be all around you, in something unusual about the product, something strange about the people who make or sell it, something rare in the way it is marketed. In some way, the product might change people's lives. Look for what will catch the journalist's attention (see below), i.e. what will appeal to their audience.

3 Develop your message

Make sure that what you are saying to the journalists is what you want to appear in print, and meets your marketing objectives as well as meeting the journalist's needs in a good story (see Chapter Four on message development).

4 Develop personalities

Make sure the brand is clearly identifiable through good design and marketing, and make sure you have executives trained and ready to speak to the press. Take suitable executives and promote them to the media as pundits – every time they are quoted you promote the brand and product.

Only when you have done the background work on the journalists, the messages and your spokespeople should you:

■ contact the journalists

■ deliver your message, in the way which appeals most strongly to each individual, with a combination of press releases, events, personal contact and meetings.

** Any approach to a newspaper, magazine or programme needs to be double-pronged. There is no point just talking to an editor, whose main task is to plan and manage the title. The editor may be responsible for commissioning features and sanctioning news stories and features, but probably writes very little. The editor needs to be aware of your product, but you also need to target those who will actually write the copy: the staff writers and freelances. **

Remember that:

- it may take time to get results

- journalists may not sit up immediately and take notice

- you may have to make several contacts before you are successful

- the more controversial and eye-catching your story, the more chance it has of being used

- you have no control over whether journalists write about your announcement, or what they write. You do the best you can, cultivate relationships, spend money on lunches and press material, and still nothing happens. Then they pick up on an angle of the story which you did not see, or did not think important

- editorial activity is extremely competitive – journalists get courted from all sides, and are being wined and dined by your competitors while you are trying to build your relationship

- you must have persistence and a long-term plan.

Research

Journalists are likely to ask you about your market and competition, so before you start any press activity you must do some research and compile statistics covering:

- the history of the sector

- other, products and competing companies

- users needs

- historical press reports and coverage

- background to the development of the new product

- case studies

- reference sites.

Collect every scrap of information relating to your product and its market.

<< Continue to monitor the market and your competitors. >>

Start with some simple 'desk research' or *secondary research*.

- Look up information at the local library.

- Collect newspaper cuttings.

- Call trade and professional bodies and collect any data they may have.

- Check your competitors' web sites.

- Pose as a customer and see how your competitors deal with you, what products you are offered, and at what prices.

- Check electronic databases for more on the competition and the market.

- Use research to identify your target press publications, programmes and journalists.

Also undertake *primary research*. Conduct a formal survey to determine response and market potential for your product.

There are two kinds of primary research: quantitative and qualitative.

- *Quantitative* is a survey of a representative sample of the public to determine statistics and measurements.

- *Qualitative* determines views, attitudes, opinions and insights and is conducted through lengthy interviews with a few people.

Telephone surveys can give a quick straw poll and feedback about how a product is doing and what people think about it.

** Commission your own consumer tracking surveys and follow the progress of products once they are in the market and being used. **

All your media messages should be underpinned by this kind of information.

** Quote your research in your media messages, particularly if it is conducted by an independent third party. **

In any research:

- questions need to be objective
- questions should not be closed, leading or ambiguous
- conclusions should be sound and relevant
- conclusions cannot be assumed from unasked questions. For example, if you discover that 50 per cent of people would like to try your product, do not assume that the other 50 per cent would not: they may not have heard of it. They may be ambivalent or have no preference either way.

What hooks a journalist's attention?

<< Ultimately, it's all about the personal relationships between you and individual journalists – relationships, relationships, relationships. >>

Your story should include at least one hook, such as:

- facts and statistics
- opinion
- controversy
- relevance
- information
- difference
- timing.

Facts and statistics

News stories are frequently based on facts or statistics because they give respectability and weight. Features more often use facts as part of the story, and to reinforce it.

Many news and feature stories use facts or statistics as the central hook. Many mention them in the first paragraph – headlines are often based around the result of a report, research or a survey. YOU SHOULD DO THE SAME. **If you've got a strong fact, use it to sell the story.** Put your story in the context of a percentage or a proportion, e.g. '90 per cent of dog owners look like their pets, says a survey by London School of Cosmetic Research' sounds better than 'lots of dogs owners look like their pets'.

** All facts have to be substantiated and preferably backed up with independent research (see Chapter Four, Message development: the facts). ******

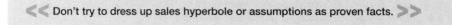

≪≪ **Don't try to dress up sales hyperbole or assumptions as proven facts.** ≫≫

** Emphasise what the facts mean to the customer – avoid the journalist saying 'So what?' ******

Journalists:

- need empirical evidence or research to underpin your claims and opinions
- know that succinct and dramatic facts make an impressive start to a news story or feature
- want to quote a creditable, independent source of their information
- know that facts and statistics help anchor a story.

Have your facts prepared. Check them. Credit the source (see Chapter Four Message development: the facts).

** ALWAYS give a credit for the source of your facts or research, and allow the journalist to contact them direct if they want to. **

<< If you are quoting a fact or statistic from a particular source, make sure that source is prepared for journalists to contact them to verify the facts. >>

Opinion

Pundits used regularly by journalists have one thing in common: they are not afraid to speak their minds.

A good interviewee has strong, controversial views and is not afraid to express them. No one who sticks too closely to the company line or is inhibited by the risk of getting into trouble will give a quote likely to be interesting and usable.

At the same time, there is no need to get yourself into trouble. Journalists love people who are indiscreet and will gossip, so be cautious of being led into saying something that you will regret. Give a balance of outspoken comment with considered verdict.

<< Preparation is the key to strong, quotable opinions. >>

Anticipate the journalist's questions and think through your responses. Write them down and talk them through so that you can give lively and interesting responses which satisfy the journalist but do not compromise you. (See Chapter Four: Message development – Opinions)

If someone rings you for an impromptu comment, err on the side of danger rather than caution. It is unlikely that you will say anything really damaging, and you might be remembered for saying something outstanding.

Controversy

The media loves drama and the essence of drama is conflict and controversy.

Bad news sells newspapers. Most news stories and many features use a negative hook or are based on a premise of conflict, e.g:

■ a report which goes against received opinion

■ someone doing or saying something unexpected and/or upsetting

■ something which somebody does not want publicised.

Journalists always 'look for an angle' which is invariably the most controversial aspect of the story – that's why you mustn't be surprised when they appear hostile.

Good journalism will stimulate debate about a controversial issue, giving different points of view and bringing all issues into the open, so the journalist looking for conflict is just doing a good job.

Anticipate this desire for conflict and suggest a controversial angle that the journalist will find interesting. This gives you control over the way the journalist uses your material, and it might distract the journalist from a more controversial angle that you do not want discussed.

There is always a risk that the journalist will not stop and will pursue the issues in a way which becomes detrimental to you, but that is a risk you have to take.

Relevance

If your story or message is not relevant to their reader, the journalist will not be interested.

Every publication and programme has a profile of its reader, viewer or listener, and its editorial contents are defined by that profile. This is usually defined in the media pack, available from the media sales team. Whatever information you give a journalist must be pitched for that 'user' or audience. Find the angle most likely to appeal to that individual's interests and needs.

Many publications state their target audience in the strapline under the title. for example, '*Network News* – the weekly newspaper for network professionals.' Look at the magazine shelves at your local newsagent: you will see that many declare their target reader on the cover.

Information

All journalists are looking for knowledge and information important to their readers.

** Information shapes opinion, and worthwhile opinions are based on clearly understood facts. **

An opinion without an informed background is virtually worthless.

Have:

- background information prepared
- explanations about technical aspects of your product
- CVs of all principals
- details of customers, prices, etc.

(See Chapter Four, Message development, for a list of facts which should be included in general information to be made available to the media.)

Difference

Journalists want something different from anything that has gone before, so list the elements that set the story apart and put them near the beginning.

** If you have once demonstrated that you understand the need for stories to be unique, journalists are more likely to come back to you in future for further comment or listen when you call again with another story. **

Do not persist in trying to interest them in stories which have no difference from previously published ones.

The difference has to be new, relevant and interesting.

** Just having a new product is not enough. **

The new product must have unique features or be dramatically cheaper or longer lasting.

Look for an angle which will interest the target audience, such as:

- the fastest
- the slowest
- the cheapest
- the biggest
- the smallest
- the first
- the last
- the most innovative
- the saddest
- the most unusual.

But without resorting to empty PR puff and hyperbole.

Back up your points of difference with facts and statistics and attributable sources. Also, learn more about your competitors and how your product can be differentiated.

Timing

Stories have to reach the right journalists at the right time.

≪ All publications have schedules, press days (when the editorial team is very busy closing the issue) and deadlines – make sure you know what they are. ≫

- It is no good giving the editor of a monthly a scoop story when the title has just closed and gone to the printers.
- It is no good giving a weekly newspaper a story which appeared in other weeklies the week before.
- Remember to give the journalists time to write the story. Few publications will hold a deadline so that a story can be substantiated or researched.

On publications and programmes which have a combination of features and news, each will have different deadlines.

- Some have long lead times (the time between the commission and the deadline).
- Others have deadlines right up to the time of broadcast or on the verge of going to the printers.
- Some, like dailies, close the evening before they appear.
- Some, like monthlies, close two weeks before the issue appears.

** When you compile your list of target publications and journalists, include details of when they require copy, deadlines, lead times and the best days to deliver information. **

When you speak to a journalist, ask what deadline they are working to, then you know whether you have time to get back later with more information.

✳✳ All magazines and newspapers always seem to be looking for readers' letters. A letter to the editor can be a quick way to editorial coverage and your name, company and web address in print. Just keep it short and snappy. ✳✳

Should you use more than one hook?

It makes sense to combine several newsworthy elements if you can. A story with more than one angle has more chance of being picked up. But don't give away all your stories in one go – save some for a second or third initiative with the media. Spread your effort and chances of editorial by spreading the hooks.

- Facts can be combined with opinion.
- Opinion can be reinforced with facts.
- Statistics can be compared with others.

✳✳ While every story should have relevance for the audience, you can also throw in some controversy. ✳✳

What is not news?

Journalists will ignore:

- only a very slight improvement to a well-established product
- 'news' that is old or has already been used elsewhere
- anything that is irrelevant to the reader, viewer or listener.

✳✳ Consider the relevance of your story, ensure it includes facts as well as opinion, has something that sets it apart from other similar product announcements, and the timing is right. ✳✳

Or ask the journalists:

> ** Few journalists mind being contacted to be asked what they are working on or whether they need opinions, facts or spokespeople to interview. **

Media personalities

Why have a personality associated with your product, brand or company?

A strong personality:

- makes the product more easily identifiable
- makes better and strong links between the customer and the product
- increases product prestige
- makes social visibility more meaningful
- creates a positive brand image in which the perception of the audience towards a particular product is positive and aspirational
- encourages feelings of expectation in the customer
- helps segment the market
- helps flag product upgrades in the future
- comforts the audience and makes a purchase feel safe
- fosters loyalty.

Think, for example, of:

- the late Victor Kiam from Remington
- Sir John Harvey Jones from ICI or the TV programme *Troubleshooters*
- Anita Roddick in connection with conscientious beauty products and marketing
- Bill Gates being synonymous with Microsoft

- Larry Ellison with Oracle
- Sir Richard Branson with Virgin
- Stelios Haji-Ioannou with EasyJet.

** Personalities are particularly useful if the product is highly technical, basically dull or obscure. **

Journalists interview the people, not the product, and people can animate issues which are worthy but dull.

Media personalities are media-astute individuals who can be relied on to be opinionated and interesting. Journalists will call upon them time and again to comment. If you or your spokespeople can achieve this position, promotion of your product will follow naturally.

The best personalities are authoritative figures at the top of the organisation.

They offer:

- a credible track record
- authority
- a breadth and depth of industry and product knowledge which creates immediate respect
- a quick and opinionated comment on a range of key issues
- a 'helicopter' perspective of the market and industry, rising above it and taking an overview, and not just focused on your product
- a vision – a practical understanding of the current situation and issues coupled with an inspirational view.

They are:

- naturally interesting
- bold
- confident

- knowledgeable
- intellectually broad and deep
- non-conformist
- charismatic
- photogenic
- articulate
- physically distinguished
- liberated from layers of management and approval – able to act on their initiative
- media trained
- media astute
- able to think on their feet.

** Sometimes 'naturally interesting' people come across as arrogant or charmless. **

Rank and position are not necessarily good indicators that an individual will be a good personality. Some senior executives freeze when with journalists or come over as hostile, while some less senior or technically minded can be eloquent and appropriate.

A good personality is a pundit who is:

- able to deliver the quick sound bites almost without thinking
- a risk-taker, unafraid of giving an outspoken view
- able to communicate the vision effectively at all levels, at all times
- visibly proactive in taking ownership of issues
- not frivolous
- not developed overnight
- able to ensure that positive messages are delivered.

The press can use a good outspoken and interesting personality in many diverse ways. They can appear:

- in profile columns
- on light entertainment programmes
- on industry chat panels
- in features or news stories.

And every time, their name or face is linked to your product.

However, the personality has to have a good understanding of:

- the product
- the competitors
- how the press works

so that they can be relied on to work confidently with the press and deliver the message the journalists and their readers want.

They will also be expected to talk about:

- the market
- the sector
- the competition
- the future.

So make sure they are prepared.

> ≪ You must be confident that the personality is not going to become involved in any scandal or negative publicity. ≫

** Make sure the media personality is skilled at dealing with unexpected questions from the press. Get them media trained and rehearse them before press interviews. **

** Raise awareness of your executives' personalities among the journalists by contacting your target media regularly and asking whether they need input to whatever they are working on and offering your executive as a pundit. **

Some journalists may rebuff you but others will want input, comment, opinion or facts.

Be prepared for the journalist to be critical of your personality – don't assume that you will be accepted at face value.

<< A strongly positive and recognisable personality appeals to customers and therefore to journalists too. >>

Journalists are also more receptive to pitches from people they know or recognise.

Media training

Putting an untrained executive in front of the media can be a terrifying experience and can create unwanted negative publicity. A media training session is the quickest way to reduce fear and build confidence and make sure you say the right things and know how to avoid saying the wrong things.

<< It can also be the quickest way to waste your budget. >>

** Journalists are looking for experts to talk to, but many experts are not naturally good at talking to the press. **

<< Journalists like people who are prepared to be outrageous, bold and outspoken, provided they are not arrogant, obnoxious or irritating. >>

Aim to train and develop your executives' skills at dealing with the press and hone their opinions so that the media regards them as personalities to be quoted.

Many journalists offer media training because it pays relatively well, compared with journalism. Some charge very little in the hope of attracting those not wanting too spend much on training.

◄◄ In media training, the old maxim applies: pay peanuts and you get monkeys. ►►

Expect to pay between £1,500 and £2,000 a day plus expenses for basic media training. No group should be larger than four or five trainees if the day is to include interview practice, although more can observe and participate. On-camera TV training, or training in a studio with lights and recording equipment, and extra journalists to give real interview practice, will add to the cost.

** Many IT and management training organisations offer media training too, but make sure the trainer has practical experience of journalism. **

◄◄ The real value of media training is the experience in taking part in 'true to life' interviews with a real journalist. The theory side of the media can seem less interesting, even though it is crucial. ►►

The quality, content and deliverables of media training courses are extremely variable, but look for:

- a background session on the way the press works
- hints and tips about what journalists are looking for
- advice on how journalists work
- information on how magazines work
- recommendations on what to avoid doing
- a workshop session to develop your message
- mock interviews to give real practice at talking with journalists and to see if you can get your message across
- references from others who have been trained.

> ** Good journalists do not necessarily make good trainers. The best have a strong aptitude and genuine enthusiasm for training combined with several years' experience of journalism. **

Be clear about what you are getting when you book.

- Some media trainers concentrate on how to dress and body language. These can be important for TV and face-to-face interviews, but the content is always more important than looks.

- Interview practice is essential, but there needs to be pre-interview training, not just a recording on camcorder.

- Others give a good balance of background briefing to the media, advice and interview practice.

- Some trainers do not have sufficiently broad experience of the trade of journalism to be able to train anyone.

- There are many media training cowboys trying to jump on the bandwagon.

- Ask in advance if you want a video recording of your interviews.

- The trainer must have a clear understanding of the issues and challenges facing each spokesperson.

- Part of media training is helping managers shape their messages so that they are media friendly.

- It saves time if you can get most of your messages worked out before the day's training so that you concentrate on role-play interview practice.

- Part of media training is encouraging people to think about the worst questions a journalist will ask and to face up to the skeletons in their cupboard. Then they can prepare and rehearse their responses.

- An external trainer who can come in cold and fresh like a journalist can offer more than in-house trainers.

- The best trainers consciously build confidence and self-esteem rather than just knocking people down and attempting to build them up again.

- Evaluation of media training is hard – long term improvement in relationships with journalists can be difficult to measure.

** Choose a trainer you can trust with sensitive information. **

For the training to be effective you need to be able to discuss the company and product strengths and weaknesses openly, frankly and in confidence.

<< If you use a working journalist, be sure that they will go off the record and not abuse your trust. >>

** The best-known journalists do not necessarily make the best media trainers. **

Different skills are required to deliver successful media training, so don't just go for the name. Look at their track record and take up references.

** Many senior managers in particular resent giving up a day for media training, but at the end of the day they invariably agree that it was time well spent. **

If you are dealing with the press on a regular basis, have a media training refresher at least once a year. (See Appendix 5 for a list of PR agencies offering media training and specialist media training contacts.)

Chapter summary

- Have a plan before you start to contact the media.
- Start with lists of target publications and programmes.
- List key staff and freelance journalists.
- Ensure you have a newsworthy angle.

- Research your market and competition.

- Develop an executive as a media personality.

- Invest in media training.

- Avoid PR puff, hyperbole or sales talk.

Case studies

Rita Brown	In-house PR assistant aged 23
Company products	SoftMicro. Educational software aimed at the 5–11 age group, plus integration and implementation services.
Target sector	IT press, home and lifestyle press.
Objective	To launch new version of product.
Action	Worked overtime on recommendation for press conference, with detailed logistics and budget planning. Advised senior executives to attend expensive hotel location to meet the press and launch the product.
Result	No journalists turned up. Twenty per cent had accepted invitations, but none turned up on the day. Rita was fired.
Recommendations	Press conferences should be held only if your company is nationally known and the news has to be announced to everyone at the same moment. Otherwise, hold a reception or one-to-one briefings with selected journalists. Expect a number of no-shows.

Suzie Ingram	Freelance journalist
Description	Suzie is 28 and recently went freelance after five years on the staff of *The Guardian*. She writes mainly for national broadsheets specialising in women's issues.
Task	To write 500 words about bankruptcies among dot.com entrepreneurs, deadline two days.
Action	Contacts her three favourite PR agencies and asks them if they have any clients with experience of bankruptcies, and views on bankrupts.
	Tries to contact several high-profile individuals whose enterprises collapsed recently.
	With six people to talk to, Suzie contacts them by email first, explaining her commission and requesting comments. Three send back detailed and extensive opinions. One other prefers a telephone interview, and two do not respond.
	She gets enough material from the email responses so doesn't need to telephone anyone. She delivers 500 words the next day.
Recommendations	Those PRs whose clients insisted on telephone interviews need to get them media trained. Increasing numbers of journalists prefer email interviews these days. With only 500 words to write, Suzie was able to finish her piece without having to talk to anyone and by taking comments delivered by email. Potential spokespeople should be ready to respond in whatever way the journalist prefers.

chapter

Your strategy

Introduction

Your media plan should include a combination of ways to reach the publications and meet the journalists to deliver your story and message.

** Attracting the journalist's eye is not easy. You are not alone in wanting the journalist to notice you and write about your product. **

A typical magazine gets several hundred press releases each day, each one from someone wanting to talk to a journalist about their product or service. The phone doesn't stop ringing with people wanting to promote their product, service or company.

You have to be:

- positive
- proactive.

And your story has to appeal (see Chapter Two for the hooks to catch the journalists' attention).

** Once one journalist starts picking up on your story you are likely to find others following suit. **

One piece of editorial can lead to others. Journalists are continually looking for the next news story.

<< Press coverage is like a rolling stone – the more you get, the more you gather. >>

Your strategy must cover:

- message development
- media planning
- media training
- looking for opportunities in the media
- planning events, meetings and interviews.

Opportunities in the media

Most publications and programmes have specific regular sections as well as news and features. They are often run by particular journalists. Select the sections most appropriate for you where you would like to see your product mentioned or your pundit quoted.

These sections include:

- product round-ups and reviews
- opinion pieces
- case studies
- contributed articles
- letters to the editor
- readers' competitions.

Product round-ups and reviews

Many publications run product reviews, tests, comparisons and recommendations. Aim to get your product included in as many of these as possible.

- Contact the editor/journalists on the title/the media sales team to establish what reviews are scheduled or planned. If there is not a suitable one, suggest it.
- Deliver the product to their office when requested or sooner.
- Make sure that the product works properly and has all documentation, leads, consumables, etc.
- Offer to set it up, install it or demonstrate how it works.
- Try to meet the journalist who will be running the review. Make it clear that you are available to help if they need it.
- Make sure they have your contact details.
- Make sure they have all other contacts, such as satisfied customers, informed analysts, other independent pundits who are familiar with the market or product.
- Don't ask for the survey results in advance – you are unlikely to be told, and it shows your inexperience.

■ Do not be surprised if the media sales team attempts to pressure you into advertising on the strength of the review. On a high-quality magazine, the review will not be affected by whether you advertise or not. On a cheap publication there may be some influence over editorial, but ask yourself: if the editorial is not independent, will people really read it and believe it?

✷✷ Don't allow yourself to be bullied into advertising. If you believe that buying advertising affects the review, question the value of the publication. ✷✷

> ✷✷ **Make sure that the editor or reviews editor has samples of your product for consideration.** ✷✷

Depending on the product, either send a review copy, a sample, or offer a demonstration.

✷✷ Don't overtly 'sell' the product's virtues. ✷✷

The journalist is probably familiar with the type of product and your competitors and will not welcome any overt sales hype. Just point out the key features and let the journalist try it out. Offer to help if they have difficulties, but otherwise leave them alone.

◀◀ Make sure that you provide all appropriate and relevant sales literature, brochures and manuals. Above all, make sure the product works perfectly! ▶▶

If a review or product round-up appears and your product is not included, contact the editor or reviews editor and politely point out the omission. By that time nothing can be done about the original editorial, but the reviews editor may consider a second editorial which includes your product.

Opinion pieces

Editors often like opinion pieces because they are free copy and allow the editorial budget to be spent elsewhere.

** Opinion pieces are an excellent way to build the profile of a personality as a pundit. **

But you have no editorial control – the copy is treated as straight editorial and will be subbed into the house style.

A good opinion piece will discuss a topical issue but not over-mention your product or company. Don't talk about the company in the body of the piece – take an issue and write a controversial, opinionated piece.

** Many freelance journalists ghost-write opinion pieces. They know the style of the publications and the copy stands a better chance of being used. **

Usually they do a telephone interview with the pundit, who will have the byline. The fee to the journalist compares favourably with the advertising rate for a similar space.

Editors will prefer you not to offer a pre-written opinion piece to more than one publication at the same time. Offer it to one, and offer it to someone else only if the first is not going to use it.

Case studies

** Case studies are excellent as a sales tool, and journalists often like to see them, but not many magazines run them verbatim because they are too bland, cosy and uncritical. **

If you have case studies written, send them to the journalists. They might pick up on a name or an example, but don't expect them to be used as they appear for sales purposes.

Many freelance journalists will write case studies for PR rates (about twice editorial rates). However, they are often uncomfortable with the lack of editorial independence or critical view.

Contributed articles

Like opinion pieces (see above), contributed articles which are most effective are not overt sales and marketing pitches but take an issue and explore it apparently independently and objectively.

Some editors like contributed articles because:

- they are free (they do not pay any fee to the writer)
- they can be contributed by a specialist or expert who knows more than a journalist.

> ** The contributed piece should not mention your company or product too overtly, but the emphasis will be on an issue or a view which is, coincidentally, connected with your product. **

Sending unsolicited work is usually a waste of time, so contact the editor before commissioning the writer, and establish that the publication does accept such pieces. You need to know the word count, whether there is a preferred topic, and anything to be avoided.

<< Have the target reader – your customer – clearly fixed in your mind, and write for them. >>

Do not offer a contributed article to more than one editor at a time. They are likely to be extremely upset if the same piece appears in other publications or programmes.

Letters to the editor

** Letters for publication are one of the most overlooked areas of opportunity for those seeking to promote their product. **

Many editors are crying out for good, entertaining, controversial letters to print. Letters pages are excellent opportunities to build name and brand familiarity.

You get:

- several column inches of your own point of view
- no criticism or comment from anyone else
- your name and company name at the end.

Avoid being too overt in promoting your product. Subtlety makes a better read and can be just as effective if you talk in an opinionated way around surrounding issues.

When you send in a letter it is worth contacting the editor to tell them that a good one is on its way, and asking whether they want a photograph of the writer.

<< When writing letters for publication: don't nag, don't argue, and never expect an apology. >>

Readers' competitions

Editors are often pleased when they can offer the readers a nice prize in a competition. They will frequently flag it on the cover, on the contents page and elsewhere, with your company name and product brand given high profile.

** Sometimes you can negotiate to receive the names of everyone who enters the competition, and these can become sales leads. **

Reaching and meeting journalists

Each of the traditional ways to reach and meet individual journalists has its advantages and disadvantages:

- press conferences
- press receptions
- one-to-ones
- workshops and seminars
- exhibitions and shows
- facilities visits
- media tours
- meals
- trips
- customer hospitality
- personal contact (see Chapter Five, Making contact).

** The blanket approach to all journalists has only limited appeal – all journalists like to be treated as individuals and expect to be. **

Find out each journalist's preference and don't offer them any other method.

Press conferences

Unfortunately, those inexperienced in media relations often think that a press conference is the essential in attracting the attention of journalists and creating editorial coverage. In fact, conferences should be used only for a major news announcement.

Press conferences are full-scale formal set-pieces, with a stage, podium, lines of organised chairs, an audio-visual (AV) system, etc.

Positive	Negative
Can result in immediate coverage	Expensive
The only way when you have a major-name client with an announcement of national or international importance which has to be conveyed to all members of the media at the same moment	Time-consuming
	A nightmare to organise and run
	Vulnerable to many external uncontrollable events which can cause havoc, e.g. strikes, weather, other events
High profile but high risk	Journalists agree to attend and then don't show up
If presenters are confident and informed, relaxed and entertaining, and the journalists enjoy themselves, they may look for the news story if they can	Outcome is impossible to control
	Freelances or journalists with travel or family commitments may avoid attending
	Journalists attending can have different levels of knowledge – attempting to interest them all can be difficult
	The image of the brand and the reputation of the organising PR can be terminally damaged if senior executives with high expectations spend several hours in an almost empty room, except for a few marginal hacks who are there only for the food, or editorial assistants
	Journalists can resent the lack of personalisation

** Do you really need one? **

** Do you really have something that newsworthy to announce? Are the journalists going to be impressed? **

What may be crucial and highly newsworthy to you may be crashingly dull to journalists.

** There are other ways to reach and meet journalists which can be far more effective and less harrowing and expensive to organise than press conferences. **

** Most journalists don't have time to attend more than a fraction of the events they are invited to. **

If you are certain that you have a reason for a press conference (and there is no better way to get your message across if it is a powerful and newsworthy story), consider:

- the date: make sure that it does not clash with press days (the date that publications close – always busy for journalists) or any other event
- the timing: mornings are best, early in the week and early in the month. Avoid press days or other obviously difficult dates
- the venue: make sure it's accessible to the journalists and offers comfort and style without being flash. You don't have to spend lots of money
- who you will invite: which journalists, which customers and which independent analysts
- the press pack (see below).

** One in five acceptances is very good, and at least a third of acceptances will not show. **

<< Journalists will be reluctant to go to a press conference which they think is just going to be a sales pitch. They are more likely to attend if they know that an independent analyst or even a biased customer will be there. >>

- Draw up a long guest list – the attrition rate is always high; 20 per cent attendance is very good, and only 5 per cent is not unusual. You will rarely get more than 50 per cent of those invited attending.

- Invite more than one journalist from each title – invite the editor, and a staffer, and a freelance who contributes regularly to that title. Leave it up to them to decide which will attend.

- Arrange for a suitable celebrity to take a major role, provided you are confident that they can handle the occasion.

- Keep your expectations low and manage the expectations of the principals.

- Give adequate notice.

- Send invitations ten days to two weeks in advance, with clear details of when, where and *what the journalists will get out of it*.

- Include a reply-paid card or fax-back form.

- Whether they reply or not, call the day before to establish whether they are still intending to come. Check that they know where the event is being held and offer to fax over a map of the location. This should give a last-minute feel for prospective attendance.

- Offer to book one-to-one interviews after the main press conference.

- Don't refuse interviews before the conference.

- Even those who confirm in advance may not show up and are unlikely to let you know.

- Unfortunately it is common practice for journalists to accept several invitations for one day, perhaps in the optimistic hope that they can cover them all.

- Have a contingency plan in case there is an unexpected event which sabotages the occasion.

- Hold a rehearsal, particularly if you have speakers who are unused to presenting.

- Don't assume anything and double-check everything.

- Make sure that all the presenters, users, experts and analysts know where they are going and what time they are supposed to be there.

- Confirm the catering, AV and seating arrangements, and have a technical run-through on the morning.

- Put out fewer chairs than number of people expected – better to have to pull out extra chairs than have chairs unfilled.

- Allow for journalists not wanting to sit too closely together (see 'Competition between journalists').

- Keep the event short, especially the formal presentation.

- Avoid sales hyperbole – you are not selling to the journalists.

- Be prepared for unexpected crises, such as the AV system breaking down, the software crashing, or a speaker calling five minutes before the start to say they can't be there in time. Have a contingency plan.

- Don't allow speakers to assume that because they are talking about this topic or product all the time, they will be fine without rehearsal. Insist that each goes through their presentation in a full dress rehearsal.

- Provide appropriate catering – a breakfast, lunch or tea. A buffet is preferable to a sit-down meal because it gives individuals more flexibility to move around to meet people, and they can leave if they need to without fuss. A formal lunch would be appropriate for a small group of similar-minded journalists, but for several dozen a buffet is more practical. *Hospitality should be good but it need not be too lavish.*

- Make space and power available for journalists to plug in their portable computer, and a direct telephone line with a modem socket.

- Don't insist on a dress code. Presenters and your executives should all be suited, but the journalists are unlikely to be.

- Have the name and job title of each presenter clearly on their desk in front of them, visible from the back of the room.

The plan for the event should be something like this.

- Arrival time ten or fifteen minutes before you want to start – no longer or you will have a group of irritated and impatient journalists.

- Sign in and refreshment on arrival. Give each a name badge. Don't be surprised if the journalists stick together and are hostile to your approaches.

- Formal presentation with product demonstration and questions kept to a minimum and as slick as possible, without gimmicks.

- Journalists are not keen on speeches. It is better to have people doing things than saying things. Have a user, analyst or other independent third party available. These should be trained and rehearsed and be prepared to answer questions from the press. Prepare them for any awkward questions which you think may arise, and rehearse their answers.

- Plan an informal session, with opportunities for one-to-one discussions and refreshments and food.

- Try not to deviate from the programme, to avoid unnerving presenters.

- Give each journalist a press pack on arrival or departure, containing:
  - press releases
  - drafts of speeches (in case they want to quote the speaker)
  - copies of the presentations
  - biographies of the speakers
  - names and contact details of all speakers, customers and analysts who attended
  - photographs of people and products
  - a complimentary copy of the product if appropriate.

- Do not include press cuttings or reprints of previous press coverage or you will kill the story dead. These show that the story is not new.

- Avoid including sales leaflets, unless they include important specifications or facts.

- Offer the journalists the option of having the contents of the press pack on CD-ROM, or having it emailed to them.

- Put the contents of the press pack on your web site.

- Don't assume that the journalists know all about your company and product – assume they don't and give them a basic backgrounder at the beginning.

- Do not overload the journalist with irrelevant material. You can omit the biographies and transcripts and say they are available on request.

- Contact each attending journalist afterwards to make sure that they have everything they want.

- Send a press pack to every invited non-attending journalist.

- Send a press pack to the rest of your journalist database, just in case it appeals to one.

** Everything said at a press conference is 'on the record' and can be published. ******

- Avoid non-disclosure agreements (NDAs) and embargoes. What's the point of telling a journalist something and then asking them not to use it? And what are you going to do if they break your 'embargo'? An NDA is a variation of the embargo and both are equally disliked by journalists. The NDA is a quasi-legal document in which the journalist agrees not to write about what they see or hear. Many journalists refuse to sign them. But although journalists don't like them, they do have their place. For a company trying to promote a story and a product, it can be useful to inform the media before the launch, yet they may not want the launch publicised before they are ready. It is also useful sometimes to give a journalist a briefing in a more relaxed atmosphere before an official launch because it gives them time to research and write the story in advance. NDAs and embargoes are requests, not enforceable commands. The question you have to ask is: What are you going to do if a journalist breaks an NDA? There are no legal sanctions you can resort to, while threatening not to give the journalist the story next time is likely to be self-defeating. A better strategy might be to give trusted journalists an 'off-the-record' briefing after you have struck an agreement that they will not use the information. However, off-the-record statements are like NDAs: you cannot be certain that the journalist will not use them, and there is nothing you can do if they break the agreement except not trust them in future.

■ A big expensive sit-down lunch is unnecessary, but refreshment and buffet on offer is appreciated.

≪ It is common practice for journalists in the US to applaud at the end of a press conference, but this is not the case in the UK. The silence at a UK press conference can be disconcerting for American executives who have not been warned. In fact, they will find it hostile. It is routine for US journalists to stand and state the publication they work for, while British journalists often just ask their question without introducing themselves. ≫

≪ Unless your company and its products touch everybody's lives every day, do not expect journalists to be beating a path to your press conference. ≫

Press receptions

A press reception is an alternative to a set-piece press conference. There may be a brief formal announcement, followed by refreshments and the journalists mingling with your staff, like a party. They are often arranged for early evening, after formal office hours, and can continue until late.

■ You need to prevent journalists only talking to each other. They can be inclined to form cliques and catch up on old times, giving PRs the cold shoulder.

■ You need to have a 'feel-good' factor so that the journalist believes they have really got value from attending.

Positive	Negative
Less formal, more relaxed.	See above under 'Press conferences' – all apply.
Allow people to mingle freely	No good for freelances, who often live out of Central London
A useful way to meet journalists you usually just speak to on the phone or contact by email. Good for relationship development	No control over unexpected external events, such as bad weather or strikes, accidents, etc., which prevent journalists attending
Good when you have a moderately well-known client with an announcement which will have impact on its sector, customers and competitors	No control over other events which clash
Good for clients who are media savvy and can cope with informal, on-the-record conversations	Freelances or journalists with travel or family commitments may avoid or be unable to attend
Useful for informal feedback from the press on their perceptions of the company, brand and product	Watch out for liggers (usually over-the-hill freelance hacks) who will come to the opening of an envelope, show no interest in the product or company, eat and drink themselves stupid, abuse the client and executives, and never intend to write anything about you, ever

- Attendance sometimes improves if journalists are offered some kind of inducement, such as a bottle of champagne or the opportunity to meet an interesting celebrity or reputable analyst.

- Offer a complimentary copy of the product, if appropriate.

- Make sure all your staff attending are media trained, not just the speakers. All staff must be prepared for any question about the product and be able to hold an impromptu interview.

- Everything is on the record.

▨ Receptions can be for several clients and can be the early evening start of a relationship-building party. PR agencies sometimes invite all their clients and all the journalists they can think of for an early evening reception which develops into a party. The clients pay for the venue and refreshments. The journalists go after work, have a drink and relax and chat to the clients. Invaluable relationships can be forged this way.

▨ Warn clients not to overtly promote their products at such a meeting. The primary objective is to get to know key journalists and create relationships. To exchange business cards with a key journalist can be your only outcome – but an excellent one.

▨ It is better not to hold a reception than to hold a poorly attended one. Have people available to 'pad out' the numbers if necessary.

▨ Follow up afterwards with each attending journalist to make sure they got everything they need, and to secure the relationship.

One-to-ones

A semi-formal meeting between one or two journalists with one or two of your staff. A one-on-one should not be six-on-one.

✱✱ Don't be tempted to face each journalist with several of your executives – it can be intimidating and off-putting for the journalist. ✱✱

Positive	Negative
An excellent relationship-building opportunity	Can require a lot of time to spend a significant session individually with key journalists
Journalists are less likely to accept and then not show up	You have to repeat the same presentation over again, removing any spontaneity
You can target your key journalists and make sure that each has their own questions answered	The journalists may not voice all their concerns and are unlikely to say that they do not understand something that you assume they know

Positive	Negative
From the journalists' point of view, they can think they have exclusive information. You can go far more in-depth for each journalist, in a way that suits them. The journalists can ask questions without their competitors hearing	If a journalist fails to turn up it is more noticeable
Good for clients which are inexperienced with the media and you need to be able to intervene in conversations if necessary	Low attendance averages by freelances who often live out of Central London
Can gear the presentation and information to each journalist's readers. Can be particularly useful when a product demonstration is necessary. A good way to gauge the journalist's reaction to the presentation, the client, the product and the message. Negative reactions can often be pre-empted	

** One-to-ones are possibly the most effective way of getting your message across and ensuring accurate editorial coverage, if you can get the journalist there. The important freelances may be reluctant. **

** Sales spiels are completely inappropriate. Make sure your sales managers know that they shouldn't try to 'sell' to the press. Get them media trained, for goodness sake. **

- One-to-ones require a short presentation and then an information question and answer session.

- Offer refreshment on arrival. Make it clear on the invitation whether a meal will also be available. Some kind of buffet or refreshment is usually appreciated.

- For economy and convenience, a lobby of a large hotel can be suitable.

- Some journalists will do one-to-ones on Sundays.

- Give the journalist a press pack to take away.

- Don't invite serious journalists to meet junior managers.

- Don't pretend something is exclusive or new if it isn't.

- Don't assume all invitations go to the editor/you only invite the editor.

- Don't tell the journalist what his readers will be interested in.

- Have something prepared to say. Do not simply invite the journalist in, sit them down and say, 'Now, what do you want to ask?' You invite the press there to tell them your story and to promote your product. Point out the newsworthy elements of the product and spell out the hook.

The best one-on-ones are with two or three journalists from publications or programmes which do not clash and four or five of your executives, and a PR person.

** Know each journalist's preference regarding one-to-ones when building your database. **

◀◀ Journalists are in continual danger of collapsing under information overload. Don't add to their problems by wasting their time with insignificant or inappropriate information. ▶▶

Workshops and seminars

Workshops and seminars are increasingly popular because they are more informal than a press conference and journalists get real value out of them – usually knowledge or information.

✳✳ When you invite the journalists, tell them what they are likely to leave the workshop knowing. ✳✳

Positive	Negative
Popular with journalists because they are good value – they get knowledge and a story	Freelances or journalists with family or other commitments may not have time to attend
You can tailor the content to meet the technical level of the group or individuals	
Good for clients with high technical knowledge	
Good for clients with little media experience who need confidence-building	

▪ For journalists, workshops and seminars are an opportunity to learn more about a specific topic from an expert on the subject. They are particularly attractive to novice journalists trying to master a complex technical topic.

▪ Workshops and seminars are best arranged for breakfast time (7am to 10am) so that the journalist can have breakfast, learn about an issue and perhaps get a story idea on the way in to work.

▪ Have a theme, such as to learn about a new technology, and have independent experts and users as well as your skilled and knowledgeable executives.

▪ Make sure that all your representatives are media trained and know how to cope with all kinds of questions from the press. It is not good enough to have a junior there with instructions not to say anything to the journos.

▪ Ensure the journalists have a chance to speak to users and others connected with the product.

■ Give a press pack of information, photographs and, if possible, a sample of the product.

■ Follow up each attending journalist to make sure they got everything they wanted and have no unasked questions, and to firm up the relationship.

Exhibitions and shows

Novices think that shows and exhibitions are good places to meet journalists. No, they are good places to launch new products to the public, but not to meet the press.

Positive	Negative
Good opportunity to meet new journalists	Specialist journalists expect to know about the product before the exhibition
Good opportunity to re-establish old contacts and relationships	Journalists might find inexperienced staff or dissatisfied customers to talk to and quote
Good for clients with executives who are experienced with the media and know when to stop selling as though they were potential customers	Sabotage tactics by competing PRs and companies can lead to dirty tricks in the press office
	Bad for clients with unrealistic expectations and no experience with the media
	Press attendance is often poor
	Journalists often slide around shows incognito and avoid meetings – they don't like being sold to
	Shows are notorious for ambushes by gushing PRs, so many journalists avoid them

- Journalists know from experience that most people working on show stands are there to sell and do not have the time to talk to the press.

- Shows can be so huge that it is difficult for the journalist to predict where they will be at any time, so they are often reluctant to make exact meeting times.

- Many journalists don't bother to go to shows because they expect to already know about the products being launched to the public.

- Press receptions are often arranged in a side room at exhibitions and announced in the press room.

- Ensure that there are enough copies of your press pack in the press office – check with the show organisers in advance to know how many journalists they are expecting. Divide the number in half (show organisers always over-estimate).

- If you want to hold a press conference, do it on the first day of the trade or consumer show – many journalists only attend the first day.

- However, the value of such conferences is dubious. You have no control over what happens elsewhere at the show or which journalists will attend the show.

- Sometimes journalists like to attend press conferences and one-on-ones to make contacts, but do not expect to get good stories.

- Journalists regard shows and exhibitions as a place to make new contacts and develop old relationships.

- Many stands offer journalists incentives such as bottles of champagne and other gifts and incentives to visit them.

- If you meet a journalist at a show, offer to take them to the bar or restaurant for refreshment – you'll get one-on-one time and a grateful journalist, particularly if you avoid talking directly about your product.

- Follow up each journalist you meet and those you don't with a call afterwards, to see if they need any information – and to secure the relationship.

Strictly speaking, the press office at shows and exhibitions should be a rest room for the media and not a place where they are plagued by marketing and PR people. The best show organisers ban PR professionals from the press office, but many allow anyone into them. As a result many journalists retire to bars rather than go into the press office where they know they will be tormented by PRs.

Facilities visits

Getting the journalist to visit your factory or shop can be a valuable opportunity to develop the relationship, but don't ask them unless they are going to get something out of it.

Positive	Negative
A good chance to develop relationships	A factory visit can be extremely dull – what are you going to do to make it interesting?
Some journalists love the chance to see how products are made or to meet users	Can be risky if the journalists sees something you'd prefer them not to see, or talks to someone not media trained
	The editor may send along an editorial assistant or junior journalist as a 'reward' for work done, with no intention of writing anything

- Combined with a product launch or new announcement, this can be a way for the journalist to get an interesting spin on the story.

- When the journalist is at the facility they will expect to be free to go anywhere and talk to anyone – they could talk to a junior clerk and find out something that you don't want printed.

- Expect to pay all the journalist's expenses, and don't use cheap travel or refreshment. If they are giving up time to be with you, they will expect to be treated well.

Media tours

Doing the rounds of the publishing houses and going to journalists' offices can be very effective. Call the publishing house and ask to book one of their meeting rooms for a day, then arrange one-on-one meetings with key journalists from that publishing house at 20–30-minute intervals. Take your own presentation equipment and arrange your own refreshments.

Positive	Negative
Excellent one-on-one relationship-building exercise	Time-consuming
It is easier for the journalists to come downstairs from their office than to travel to a press reception or meeting elsewhere	Journalists can still be hard to see – you can spend a long time waiting in reception
	Journalists can agree to come down from their office but then still be too busy to spare the time
You can meet several journalists in one visit	
Can be particularly useful when a product demonstration is necessary	Can be difficult to get a foot in the door – not all publishing houses allow them
A good way to get an unknown client or a product with limited appeal in front of key journalists	Because they are on their home turf, the journalists may feel particularly free to ask incisive, difficult or plain rude questions
	You only meet staffers, whereas freelancers can be more important

- Avoid a sales pitch but make some kind of presentation and then invite questions.
- Can be embarrassing – the journalists can simply ignore you.
- Don't hint at a story when you invite the journalists – tell them what the story will be.
- You'll probably need to lure them down from their offices upstairs, either with a really impressive new product or technology (remember the 'So What?' factor – journalists can be very hard to impress) or food or gifts.

■ Make sure the touring executives are media trained and know how to deal with difficult questions, and to think on their feet to tailor each presentation to the journalist.

** You can't do too much preparation for a media tour – the journalists will expect you to know everything about their publications, and what they are personally responsible for writing. **

Meals

Journalists often appreciate being taken out for a drink or a meal, provided they are not subjected to a heavy sales pitch. Can be breakfast, lunch or evening, depending on the journalist's preference.

Positive	Negative
Excellent one-on-one relationship-building exercise	No control over whether the journalist writes a story, or what they will say
You can find out more about the individual journalist and how they like to work	Everything is on the record
Good for giving background information	The journalists can take delight in accepting your hospitality and then proving that they cannot be 'bought' by writing nothing
You can tailor your content to each journalist and their audience	Not good when a product demonstration is required
Can result in long-term positive editorial coverage	Key journalists and freelances may not have time to spare
	The environment can be noisy and unconducive to a business meeting.
	Watch out for liggers and freeloaders
	Not necessarily a good way to get instant coverage

- Do not spend the whole time talking about your product. Mealtime is equally effectively spent talking about wider issues and what the journalist is looking for.

- Regard a meal meeting as an opportunity to get to know the journalist better, not as a chance to ram your product down their throat.

- Have no expectations of any editorial as a result of a meal.

- US journalists are often not allowed to accept such hospitality, or gifts or trips, because it is regarded as unethical and opens them to corruption. This is not the case in the UK and you will be expected to pay all the journalist's expenses.

- A meal is only an attempt to bribe if you try to keep it secret.

** Don't expect the journalist to pay, unless they are American, in which case, if they want to, let them go Dutch. **

Trips

Taking journalists on all-expenses-paid jaunts can be an extremely useful and cost-effective way of building relationships.

- Manage expectations. A trip will not necessarily lead to immediate positive coverage. At best, it might only raise the journalist's awareness of your company and brand.

- Be selective about who is invited.

- Be prepared for a key journalist to accept and then for a substitute to turn up on the day without prior arrangement. Many publications 'divvy out' the trips as a reward to junior staff. If that happens, be pragmatic – today's junior may be tomorrow's editor. Look upon it as a chance to develop a relationship with someone early in their career.

- Expect to pay for everything. The journalist should not have to pay for any extras.

Positive	Negative
Excellent way to develop and build relationships	Journalists can take advantage of your hospitality and print nothing, or print something negative – you have no control and they will not necessarily feel obliged to you
Cost-effective way to ensure long-term, favourable attitude,	Can be expensive
	Can take too much time
	Not necessarily a good way to get instant coverage
	Very exhausting for the organising PRs – you are on duty the whole time
	If the journalist doesn't have a good time they can blame you or end up with a negative view of the company or brand
	The journalists can regard trips as a 'jolly' – a freebie, an opportunity to help you spend your profits before the taxman takes his slice
	Freelances are unlikely to have the time to go
	The editor may send along an editorial assistant or junior journalist as a 'reward' for work done, with no intention of writing anything

Customer hospitality

If you are taking a group of customers to a special event, such as a sporting or arts event, one or two key journalists can be included in the party.

■ Make sure that all your customers are happy about journalists being present – it means that they may be misquoted or quoted inappropriately.

Positive	Negative
Excellent way to develop and build relationships	Journalists can take advantage of your hospitality and print nothing, or print something negative – you have no control and they will not necessarily feel obliged to you
	Everything is on the record, even your customers' comments

Personal contact

Media relations is all about relationships, so the method and frequency of your contact with your key journalists can be critical. Annoy them and the relationship can be dead.

Positive	Negative
You can tailor what you deliver to meet each journalist's needs and preferences	If you get it wrong you can alienate a key journalist and it can be extremely hard to repair the damage

- Never contact a journalist unless or until you are familiar with their work and who they write for.
- Be flexible and use the most suitable/preferred method for each.

Ways of initiating personal contact are:

- *telephone* – journalists can be rude. They resent cold calls
- *post* – journalists might not respond. Press releases can be binned without being opened
- *email* – the preferred choice, but keep it simple (see Chapter Seven, Computer-aided journalism)

- *fax* – dated
- *web sites* – useful. Many journalists have their own, with email links.

> ** Journalists are busy and although they want to hear about new stories and interesting opinions, they won't tolerate having their time wasted. Make sure you have something worthwhile to say. **

- Make sure you have an up-to-date database on each journalist and their preferred method of contact. Some like emails for contact but snail-mail press releases, others like telephone calls.
- If you haven't got their attention in the first few seconds, they won't wait to see what's coming next.
- First catch their attention. Then create interest by explaining how your product is relevant. Turn the interest into a desire to hear more and promise action in the form of a demonstration of the product or an interview to discuss it.
- If you really believe you have a good, newsworthy story, pitch it three times to a journalist before you give up. Email, send the press release, then follow up with a telephone offer of information, quotes or an interview. If the journalist doesn't show interest, forget it.

<< Prolonged attempts to initiate contact with a journalist who doesn't respond are a waste of your time, and can alienate the journalist. >>

** Once you have contact with a journalist, or have met them, keep the relationship alive with further conversations or meetings, but only when you have something to say. **

> << The key to achieving successful editorial is getting the right information to the right people at the right time. >>

Competition between journalists

If you see a group of journalists together they can appear to be getting along fine, but there is likely to be an undercurrent that is invisible to you: journalists working for different publications or programmes are in direct conflict and are therefore highly competitive.

- They don't like going to small press meetings together.
- They don't always like sitting near to each other.
- They are defensive and protective about the angle they intend to take on a story.
- They might appear to socialise and get on well – up to a point.
- They don't want other journalists to know what they know.
- They are secretive about their contacts and are reluctant to reveal their sources of information.
- They won't ask questions in an open press conference that will give other journalists from competing titles any indication of their angle, or answers that they want exclusively.

** Journalists can be silent in an open press conference and not ask any questions but want a private one-on-one meeting afterwards. **

- If you are sending out invitations to small press events, be aware of any potential conflict between members of the press, either personal or professional.
- At a large conference any rivalry or antagonism can usually be absorbed, but you can have problems if you invite journalists from titles which are in direct competition to a small press lunch or a seminar.
- Journalists from directly competing titles will be unwilling to discuss the product or to question you in front of the others so that the other journalists don't learn anything specific from the debate.

- If one journalist has a particular angle they will be reluctant to give the competition any clue about the approach they want to take, and will remain silent and in ignorance rather than give the competitor an idea about the way they are thinking.

- Journalists who are in direct competition, either in the titles for which they work or the areas which they cover, appreciate discreet one-to-one briefings rather than larger groups where several of their competitors are also present.

- It is usually okay to invite several journalists who do not compete directly for a small lunch briefing.

- Some journalists like to show off their knowledge and interrogation skills in front of their peers.

One way to deal with competition between journalists is: *ignore it*.

- Aim to treat every journalist and publication equally.

- Don't give any preference or advance information to any one title or individual.

- Ensure complete even-handedness in giving out information, pictures and products for review.

** Some companies select preferred journalists and titles and give them special advance knowledge, pictures or products, hoping that the selected journalists will choose to regard the 'special' briefing as a scoop and give the story high-profile coverage. **

This strategy can fail dramatically – and then what do you do?

- First, the selected journalists may not rise to the bait and choose to ignore the product or give it scant coverage.

- Second, the other journalists may feel affronted and not report it at all, even when they are given all the information.

Consequently 'advance briefings' are a risky and complex strategy and are not recommended. Trying to 'play off' the journalists against each other, or trying to secure high-profile editorial coverage by promising exclusives in this way, frequently backfires.

Editorial, advertising and advertorial

You must recognise the clear boundaries between editorial, advertising and advertorial. If you get them confused, you are unlikely to be successful in promoting your product to the media. If the publication gets advertising and editorial confused, ask yourself whether the publication or programme is worth appearing in – it is unlikely to have credibility among the target audience.

Publishing houses and their products vary, but as a general rule there is a wide gulf between advertising and editorial. Often the editorial and advertising teams are physically kept apart to emphasise the separation.

- The editorial staff are often sensitive about pressure from advertisers and the advertising department.
- Know the difference and operate between the two groups sensitively.
- Keep your dealings with the media sales team clearly separate.
- Do not attempt to leverage your advertising spend by directly pressuring the journalists to include your product, mention your company or quote your executives because you are buying advertising space.
- Understand the differences between advertising and editorial, the different personality types of the two teams, and their different objectives.
- Don't treat editorial staff like media sales staff.

In reality, with many publications partially or wholly dependent on advertising revenue, there is often considerable collaboration between the advertising and editorial teams. This may be covert or overt, discreet or obvious.

** The closer the advertising and editorial, the less credible the editorial and the less appeal it has to the discerning reader – your potential customer. **

Titles which promise editorial in exchange for advertising are often barely worth reading. The editorial content of those titles will reflect the cosiness in non-critical editorial full of meaningless PR puff. In those titles there are no respected independent views and opinions. You should ask yourself: 'If I can buy editorial coverage by paying for an advertisement, is the editorial worth having?'

** Most editorial teams produce a features list for the media sales teams to sell advertising. You can use these lists to try to get to talk to the right journalist at the right time to ensure that you are mentioned in a feature. But this is a risky method to rely on – often the copy is delivered before the features lists are released, and the lists are liable to change. **

Advertorial

The grey area in between advertising and editorial is advertorial. Publications vary on how the advertorials are handled and how many they accept. Some are completely controlled by the media sales team. The worst appear in the same style as editorial copy. If you are offered the opportunity to write your own editorial, question the credibility of the title.

Editors have mixed feelings about advertorials.

- They free up editorial budget.
- But they can compromise the editorial independence.

Editors will aim to edit and control the advertorials so the readers are not confused about whether they are reading copy that has been paid for.

- Advertorial can be used to raise your profile as a pundit, launch you as an expert, increase awareness of the product and increase sales gradually.

- Advertising should be used if you want to announce specific offers or products, inform your customers about your product or increase sales immediately.

- Advertorial is often written by freelance journalists who charge the PR company at least twice the normal journalistic rates for creating copy which the editor will accept and the reader will perceive as genuine editorial.

- Aim for editorial for best credibility.

- For best cost effectiveness, combine advertising with other marketing, PR and personal contact efforts to persuade journalists to write or talk about your product.

- The message that you give the press should be reinforced by the advertising, although the two efforts should be quite separate.

- Advertorial does not necessarily cost less than advertising.

- Advertorial can provide you with apparently independent credibility.

- Depending on the publication, you can have reasonable or even complete control over what appears on an advertorial page.

- Advertising has lower credibility among the readers.

- Advertising is the most straighforward and easiest way to be sure of what appears – you have absolute control and you can say what you like, provided the message is, in the words of the Advertising Standards Authority, 'decent, legal, honest and truthful'.

- Editorial costs little except PR costs and executives' time.

- Editorial offers no control over what appears.

The advertising/editorial relationship

Media sales and editorial people often have distinctly different personalities.

- Media sales people need a hide like an elephant and considerable chutzpah to keep telephoning people who don't want to know.
- Media sales staff have to be tough and determined.
- Media sales staff are trying to meet targets by selling advertising space.
- Editorial staff are more creative and sensitive.
- Editorial staff seek to educate, entertain and inform the audience.
- Editorial staff are less likely to seek you out, while a media sales person will.
- Media sales people sometimes pose as editorial, or are unclear in stating at the beginning of a call which team they are from, to get your attention.
- The two groups rarely socialise.
- They are often located in different parts of the publishing house. This is healthy. Too much collaboration between the two teams can lead to pressure on journalists, which leads to biased copy which lacks objectivity and independence.
- The degree of contact and influence between advertising and editorial can vary between publishing houses and even between different titles in the same publishing company.
- The level of influence and contact is often driven by the editor – a strong editor will ensure separation. At one extreme there is absolutely no contact, no features list, no feedback or flow of information from one side to the other. At the other, the two departments are closely linked.
- You may be asked to pay 'colour separation costs' to make sure that your press release is used in the editorial pages. If so, question the value of the publication. If it is obviously covert advertising and you can see it, so can the readers.

Even on titles where there appears to be a clear separation between editorial and advertising teams, it is not uncommon for the editor and the sales manager to have regular meetings at which:

- the editor tells the advertising sales team leader certain useful things, such as what features are coming up over the next 12 months and which companies are mentioned in editorial
- the editor will tell the sales team manager exactly who is quoted and what is said, and even let them see copy
- the advertising sales manager may request that certain companies, people or topics are mentioned, which will give them leverage for media sales activity.

** Can editorial be influenced if you advertise? Possibly, but you should never mention your advertising spend to the journalist – it is guaranteed to antagonise. **

- If you want to leverage your media spend, do it through through the advertising team and not with the editorial team.
- Threatening to withdraw your advertising if the editorial fails to mention or quote you is usually an empty, useless gesture, even on those publications where there are strong links between the teams. Many journalists even take pleasure in not mentioning advertisers if they feel that they are under pressure – it demonstrates their editorial independence.

** A good editor is a strong editor, willing and able to stand up to advertising pressure in the name of editorial independence. Those publications which have weak editors who give in to heavy pressure from the advertising team soon lose the respect of the readers, because they can see when the editorial begins to lose its independence. Gradually the publication loses its good name, and it becomes read less and less. Eventually, it loses its advertisers because none of the potential readership bothers to pick it up or believes the editorial content. It has no value and, unless the slide is checked, it will eventually close. It is important for the long-term survival of the publication that there is separation between the advertising and editorial teams. **

✳✳ In some industries and sections of the media, advertising and editorial are strongly linked and journalists have very little freedom to be critical. These are not generally respected either by the journalists or, more importantly, by the target audience, your potential customer. **✳✳**

Colour separation charges

There is growing trend among some magazines to charge for 'colour separation' to ensure that press releases are used. The charge is allegedly for the cost of printing colour, and you have to 'pay or stay off the page'.

- Only magazines with low credibility or respect attempt colour separation charges.

- Any respectable magazine discusses colour separation as part of the advertising package, never in connection with editorial.

- Any publication that will select its contents according to who will pay colour separation costs will have little value among the readership.

- Some magazines promise editorial coverage when colour separation costs are paid – again, because of the lack of editorial independence, it will have no credibility.

- Refusal to pay colour separation costs will ensure that your budget is spent on more worthwhile media activity.

Opinion pages

Positive	Negative
Excellent way to build an executive's profile as a pundit	Can be difficult to place – editors don't take many per issue.
Excellent way to get a company or product message over direct to the target customer or audience	Require considerable research to ensure that the content meets the needs of the reader
	Require considerable effort investment for risk of no exposure

- The copy is contributed by the 'advertiser' but they do not pay for it to appear.

- It is arranged with the editorial team and comes under the editorial page count.

- Opinion copy is submitted to the editorial team as if it were written by a journalist. (Freelance journalists often work with PR agencies to deliver opinion copy which is acceptable to the editor, and meets the house style and the needs of the audience.)

- Opinion pages are treated like other editorial copy, are subbed and put into house style.

- The editor has complete control over the content.

- The sub-editor will take out any excessively flattering references to the company or product.

- Be subject specific, not client or product specific. Be content with the byline and contact details at the end.

- Opinion pages are subject to the vagaries of editorial pressure and are often dropped at the last minute or held over. Editors use them as 'fillers' if they need last-minute copy.

- Often best when dealing with intangibles and concepts, like support or maintenance, product returns or sales techniques.

> ** Monitor the climate in the sector and prepare your spokespeople with some topical and outspoken views – then sell the idea to the editor. **

Aim:

- to deliver contributed copy which is not full of promotional puff
- to deliver copy which is as objective and independent as possible
- for copy which is opinionated and controversial, debating topical issues
- for a well rounded, well written, well argued discussion.

** Writing opinion pages can be a cheaper, and more effective way of promoting your product. **

Arrange opinion pieces in advance with the editor. They will only accept one if it fits in with editorial plans.

Pre-written opinion pieces should be circulated with care – if the same one appears simultaneously in several publications you can cause long-term damage to your media relations.

<< For details of advertorial, contact the advertising sales manager. To discuss opportunities for contributed editorial, contact the editorial team. >>

Using case studies

Some publications like to use case studies because they are a cheap way to fill space and can illustrate a point to the reader. Readers also like to read about people like themselves.

However, case studies are essentially a sales tool. They are not usually suitable for editorial because:

- they are too full of PR puff
- they are written by a committee
- they are too bland
- there is never anything negative or critical in them.

However, many journalists like to read case studies and it is worth sending them along with the press releases. It is rarely worth writing an editorial case study on spec – first agree with the publication that they want one and then commission a freelance journalist to write it.

✳✳ If you send a case study to a journalist, make sure that the individuals mentioned are prepared and happy for a journalist to contact them as a result – the journalist may be interested in the basic case study but want to 'flesh it out' with their own research. ✳✳

◄◄ There is nothing more annoying for a journalist than to be sent an interesting case study but then to find that the subject is unwilling to talk to the press. What a waste of time! ►►

Media train the subjects of any case studies in case journalists pick up on the story, want to use it and want to talk to those involved in the case study. If the case study subjects are untrained they can easily mention problems which were actually slight, but can easily be blown up out of all proportion.

Chapter summary

- Failure to plan is planning to fail.

- Have a strategy, a plan and tactics. Don't just write a press release and send it off.

- Decide which method, or combination of methods, is best for you to contact journalists: press conferences, receptions, one-to-ones, etc. Build a database on each journalist and note which ways they prefer to be contacted.

- Only contact a journalist if you have a good reason.

- Advertising has no effect on editorial (or if it does, you should question the value of the publication).

- Advertorial can give you more control over the editorial content – up to a point.

- Opinion pieces offer excellent control over editorial, if the editor wants to publish them. Make them controversial for maximum chance of being used.

- Prepare case studies for sales purposes and send them to journalists for interest, but only if the subject is prepared for the journalist to contact them to discuss things further and be quoted.

Case studies

John Price	PR executive aged 29
Company	OnMessage.com, a mid-sized PR agency with 80 employees including 15 PR executives.
Clients	IT and telecoms. John is responsible for two telecoms clients.
Target sector	IT and telecoms trade and user press.
Objectives	To ensure that journalists know about the latest version of the products, and to get them reviewed.
Action	Checked the list of target journalists and publications and ensured that it was up to date. Wrote a draft press release for client approval. Contacted those publications that carry product round-ups and reviews. Delivered full working copies of the product to key journalists, for them to use and keep. Followed up with emails and telephone calls to check each journalist had everything they needed, and was able to use the product without problems.
Result	Out of 15 target publications, 12 carried either small reports on the news page or full product reviews.
Recommendations	Good action with good response. It only remains for John to follow up with the journalists who didn't report on the product, to offer to take them out to lunch so that they still learn about the product, and to contact those journalists who did cover the product, to maintain and develop the relationship. Start planning a press reception with users and analysts in a couple of months' time.

Michael Power	Features Editor, *What Computer System?*, aged 27
Description	Michael writes and commissions features of interest for this monthly trade magazine for system integrators and computer system resellers.
Task	To manage a section in a forthcoming issue on WAP phone technology. Will write one feature himself, and commission three freelances to write four other features.
Experience	After a conversation with the media sales team, Michael draws up a list of features and topics to be covered.
	Contacts three freelances he knows he can rely on and asks them to write the content, apart from the lead feature, which he will write. He cannot use freelances to write all the words because his budget is small.
	He writes one feature and the freelances deliver their copy two weeks later.
	Michael reads through all the copy, ensures that all contact details are in place, signs off the invoices and delivers the copy to the sub-editor.
	The supplement appears two months later.
Recommendations	The best PRs are in regular contact with Michael and knew that he was planning a WAP applications supplement. They made sure that he and the commissioned freelances had all the information about their products, plus emailed quotes and comments from key spokespeople.
	Michael and the freelances were able to write the copy easily because all the material was 'fed' to them in good time before their deadline.

4

Develop your message

Introduction

It is madness to approach a journalist without any preparation. You should know the journalist, their publication or programme, their preferred ways of working, their foibles, likes and dislikes. It is also crucial to have your message and angle ready and know what the story and hook will be.

** The message you give to the journalist should be the one that you want to see appear in the media, and the one you want your potential customers to see. **

** 'Be prepared' is not just a Scout's motto. If you want positive editorial coverage, it should be yours too. **

- It is a surprisingly short step from what you say to the journalist to what appears on their computer screen and then what is read by their reader, your potential customer.
- You have more control over what appears in the press than you think.
- The journalist will be looking for controversy, conflict and opinion: give that to them and you are doing your best to ensure that what appears is what you want your customers to read, while satisfying their craving for a good story.

> ** The journalist is looking for a fresh story of interest to their audience. You are looking to promote your product and company. The two are not necessarily incompatible. **

Why have messages ready?

You have no direct control over what journalists print, but they are unlikely to deliberately and mischievously misquote you. What you tell them is likely to be what they print. Having a message prepared is the best way to say what you want to appear.

<< There is no point in having a meeting or interview with a journalist without giving thought in advance to what you want to say. >>

** Talking to a journalist without preparing first is like taking a step into the hungry lions' cage when naked. At least try to wear some armour and take a mobile phone. **

- Talking to the press without thinking though your messages in advance is almost certainly going to end as a wasted opportunity.

- When they talk to the press, even the most experienced pundits can feel flustered and forget what they want to say, and what they want to avoid talking about.
- Have your messages prepared and then look for opportunities to present them.

Refining your messages

Your message is the product's positive marketing sales slogan or your sales objectives. An interview is your opportunity to get your product message across. And you can shape the impression your potential customers have because journalists will often use the words you use.

Your messages have to have:

- credibility so that the journalist has confidence in the message and belief in you
- appropriate context for the journalist and programme or publication
- the right content, appropriate for the viewer, listener or reader
- clarity so that the message is unequivocal
- continuity with previous and proposed press activity
- impact so that they are remembered.

When writing your messages:

- make the message snappy
- use pointed phrases
- use imaginative comments
- accentuate the positive
- personalise them
- avoid clichés
- avoid sales puff

- back them up with facts, specifications and statistics
- don't qualify them but enlarge upon them or develop them
- make the main points newsworthy
- focus on the emotional needs of your potential customers
- emphasise messages based on benefits to the reader or listener
- look for the unique selling points of your product and use them as part of the message
- draw the journalist's attention to what is novel or newsworthy
- avoid gratuitous 'latest' or 'newest' or other glib and trite descriptions unless they are demonstrably true
- describe your product in terms of what it will do and refer to the difference that the product will make
- focus on what makes the product interesting and irresistible
- describe the impact that this product will have on people's lives
- describe the way that the product will change a process
- describe the benefits your product will bring
- avoid empty hyperbole
- build messages based on your track record and long-term objectives.

** Only refer to a product as the 'fastest' or 'cheapest' if you are sure that it is and have facts and statistics to back up your claim. **

Message development part one: the facts

Start with what you know – the facts.

** When you are talking to the press you are representing your organisation – you are expected to know all the facts about it. **

Failure to know basic facts reflects badly on you and your enterprise. Invest effort in making sure you have as many facts at your fingertips as possible.

<< Be ready to back up every statement with a statistic, facts or figure. >>

** The journalist will feel free to ask anything even vaguely connected with product, your market, its sector and your competitors. They might also ask personal questions which, in another context, might seem rude. **

Have all possible facts and statistics ready relating to:

- your product
- your target market
- the competition
- their products
- their market share
- new products coming down the line from your competition and from yourself
- past and projected turnover
- past and projected targets for revenue and growth
- the size of your company
- whether you will be recruiting, by how many and what the new employees will be doing
- the size of the market and its projected growth.

** You also need to be able to put all facts into context, interpreting them for the journalist in the broad picture. **

> << It is as important to know as much about your competition as your own products and company. >>

- Simplify all figures by rounding up or down to the nearest whole number, reducing fractions and decimals to nearest whole numbers and only using one or two numbers as examples.

- Use percentages wherever possible, which is often the most graphic way of putting a figure across.

- Use graphs where you can, and any other visual representation of your figures and statistics.

QUIZ: DO YOU KNOW ALL THE FACTS?

Question:	Answer:
What is the legal name of your company?	
How you describe it in ten words or less without using any hyperbole or PR puff (don't use 'the leading' but just describe what the company does)?	
When was it founded?	
What accreditations or certifications does the company have?	
What awards has it won?	
Give a complete list of brand names or products or services.	
What are the trade prices?	
What are the end-user prices?	
What are its routes to market (i.e. direct, wholesale, distributor network)?	
What percentage goes through each channel?	
How does it manage the different channels and differentiate between them without channel conflict?	

Question:	Answer:
What new products are coming through from R&D?	
When will they be launched?	
What were last year's sales by volume or number of units?	
What were last year's sales by revenue?	
What is this year's target by volume or number of units?	
What is this year's target by revenue?	
What is the overall size of your target market by units?	
What is the overall size of your target market by revenue?	
Describe your target market.	
What is your current share of the market?	
What is your position in the market?	
Who are your main competitors?	
Which are your top customers?	
How many staff do you have?	
How many staff are being recruited this year?	

** Every spokesperson should know which facts are not to be given to the press, and have a clear and acceptable reason why that data is confidential. (See Dealing with journalists' questions.) **

In addition, use a SWOT analysis to determine the facts about the company and the strengths, weaknesses, opportunities and threats of its products and services.

	Company	Product
Strengths		
Weaknesses		
Opportunities		
Threats		

This can also help you prepare for the worst questions that a journalist might ask.

To help develop your messages based on the facts, draw the following matrix:

	Fact	Sales message	Media message
Company			
Products			
Services			
Employees			
Customers			

Take each fact from the quiz and from the SWOT analysis and put it in the appropriate box according to whether it relates to the company, product, services, employees or customers. Fill in the grid. Extrapolate each fact into a sales message and then a media message. These might be the same – you need to use your judgement to decide whether the sales message is too full of hyperbole, puff and unsubstantiated hype.

Use the FAB acronym:

- F = Facts
- A = Advantages (it delivers)
- B = Benefits (to the customer)

to help arrive at the media messages.

Ideally, you should have two or three media messages in each category. These can be a few short words, or a sentence long, provided they are succinct, startling, novel, original and interesting.

For example, if the company was founded in 1940, the message could be that the company is well established. If the company was founded in 1999, the message could be that the company is new and dynamic.

Be clear which are sales messages and which are media messages – journalists don't like to be sold to. Sales messages can be full of puff. Media messages should concentrate on user benefits.

Use customers and reference sites to reinforce your messages. Ask satisfied customers to give a few sentences on the benefits they have derived, and their return on investment (ROI), for example. A list of these testimonials, with the company they come from and ideally a contact name too, should be available to all journalists.

** Mention the company name and brand names as often as possible. **

** Think that you are 'creating the quote' when developing your messages. Think of the text on the page. **

Message development part two: the issues

If you have any awareness of what journalists want, you will have realised already that the facts are not what journalists are really looking for. They are more to support your message than be the message itself.

** If you focus on the facts alone the journalists will be quickly bored. **

They also want comments and opinions.

So you have to:

- first identify the issues and topics that the journalists and their readers are interested in
- then develop controversial, interesting messages on each topic.

Issues	Comments, views and opinions
1.	
2.	
3.	
4.	
5.	
6.	

Identify the issues by reading the press and talking to customers. Become a thought-leader by identifying issues before they become widely developed – journalists and editors are keen to be the first to discuss and air a new issue.

Issues might include:

- a skills shortage
- training issues
- new legislation
- new technology
- the impact of the internet
- security
- mergers and acquisitions
- management techniques
- customer satisfaction
- logistics.

** Know which are your personal opinions and which are the company's view. **

- Be as outspoken and controversial as you can.
- Keep your opinions short, sharp and snappy.
- Before you start giving your opinion, be clear who the audience is going to be.

** Mention the company name and brand names as often as possible **

Message development part three: anticipating journalists' questions

✳✳ Leading politicians and captains of industry routinely have a 'what are they going to ask us today' session with their PR and communications staff every morning or before meeting the media. It is not rocket science to imagine what the top questions will be. The PR staff role-play the executive and fire the questions, working through the responses until they are the best answer, and then rehearsing and rehearsing their response until it is word perfect and appears spontaneous. Not to do so would be madness. ✳✳

Create a chart of predictable questions and your best response.

Predictable questions	Best response
1.	
2.	
3.	
4.	
5.	
6.	

Take the facts from the quiz and SWOT analysis and turn each into a predictable question, e.g. your company was founded in 1940 – how can such an ancient enterprise understand the modern customer's buying patterns and needs?

Or your company was only founded a year ago – that's not very long, is it? Or, how can such a young company understand the market or hope to compete against established competitors?

** For every fact there is a positive message and for every positive message there is a negative one that the journalist will think of. **

> ** By anticipating what the journalist might ask, you can respond positively and emphasise the positive virtues and benefits of the company and product. You will be more credible as an interviewee and eliminate the possibility of being 'tripped up' by the journalist. **

- Anticipate contentious issues and difficult questions.
- Assume that the journalist has done background research before speaking to you.
- Assume they know about all the skeletons in the company's cupboard.

Include questions about:

- your competitors and their problems ('I'm not in a position to comment on our competitors' problems')
- your new products ('Unfortunately I'm not able to talk about that yet for competitive reasons, but I can assure you that as soon as we are ready to go public you will be the first to get the story')
- the skeletons in your cupboard ('Those problems are behind us now' or 'All that happened a long time ago and we have moved forward now')
- weaknesses in the company or its products ('Having a young management team helps us keep in touch with the market' or 'We have plenty of older executives to bring experience to the team').

◀◀ There is always a positive answer to every negative point without being evasive. The trick is to anticipate the negative and critical questions and think through the best response. ▶▶

There are standard responses to difficult questions – See Chapter Six on interviews.

- There is no excuse for allowing yourself to be stumped for an answer when you have time to prepare.
- This doesn't mean that you should think of lies.
- Consider how frank you want to be on certain topics.
- You need to be able to deal with the worst possible questions.
- You can avoid being led into a question area that you'd rather avoid.
- If you really don't want to answer a question there are proven responses which can gracefully deflect the journalist without arousing curiosity.
- A charming reply can prevent a journalist digging further in a sensitive area.

** Often the journalists don't mind being taken down another path. All they want is a good story, and even though they recognise it is happening, they may allow it to happen. **

◀◀ Even the worst kind of terrier journalist can recognise when an interviewee is not going to give any more on a particular topic and will move on to something else. ▶▶

- A journalist will take the position of devil's advocate, regardless of their personal opinions.
- Whatever you say, whatever claim you make, you can expect the journalist to criticise, make a counter-claim or ask you to defend your position in some way.
- The last thing a journalist will do is accept everything you say at face value.

- The journalist may even take several perspectives on your position, 'changing hats' and taking different points of view against yours.

- Don't take this personally: the journalist is just doing their job.

- They are just trying to clear a way through your promotional puff and sales hyperbole to the facts.

- Aim to be natural and relaxed rather than guarded and defensive.

- Rehearse your answers so that you are smooth in delivering them and reassuring in your response.

◄◄ Rehearse, rehearse, rehearse, and your responses will be more plausible and credible. ►►

- Role-play repeatedly.

- Ask your colleagues to play the part of an investigative journalist asking the worst questions they can imagine.

- See how well you can fend them off, move the conversation on and deliver the messages you want to see in print.

✱✱ Mention the company name and brand names as often as possible. ✱✱

Evolve your messages

You don't only want press coverage when the product is new – refresh your messages regularly to match changes in the company and the changing product life cycles.

✱✱ Editorial press coverage is not just for launches – media activity should continue throughout the product's life cycle, changing with it. ✱✱

<<< A new product needs different messages from one which has been on the market for a while. >>>

Use the Boston Matrix as a guide to how your messages should change to match each stage of the product life cycle.

- When the product is very new and only being bought by innovators or trend-setters, the marketing and PR need financial and energy investment. You have to introduce the product with messages of novelty, leading edge and breaking new ground. Aim to generate customer interest, stimulate desirability, and encourage pioneering purchasers.

- As the product begins to be accepted but is still in its growth stage, you need greater emphasis on expert opinion being persuasive rather than informative. As the product achieves wider consumer acceptance, new features and price cuts can be introduced.

- As the product moves into the third stage of maturity and becomes a commodity, aim to emphasise user case stories. Maintain the differential between your product and others through lower price, improved product features or extended warranty. Sales will stabilise as the market becomes saturated and competition may increase as other firms enter the market. Other products in the market can help yours, giving you new messages.

- As the product moves into its final stage of gradual decline and sales begin to fall, cut back the press focus and shift your primary press activity to newer versions or fresh products – but don't forget the original product. It demonstrates longevity and is a positive message. You can also revive and relaunch the original product through repositioning or repackaging.

Cue cards and crib sheets

Once you have established your messages, be ready to be proactive about getting them across to the media. You need to be familiar with your messages and opinions or have them at hand.

■ Transfer your messages to cue cards, crib sheets or some other form of *aide mémoire*.

■ Have them handy in your desk in case a journalist telephones unexpectedly.

■ Read through messages, issues and opinions before an interview or meeting with the press.

■ Every individual likely to talk to the press, either formally or informally, should have a cue card or crib sheet handy, so that if a journalist calls they have their messages ready.

Revise your messages and rewrite your cue cards/crib sheets on a regular basis, at least every three or four months. Otherwise you will be saying things that have already appeared in the press and the messages will be dated. In particular, revise and rewrite the opinions on topical issues and the obvious anticipated questions.

Have your messages pinned up on notice boards around the building so that all staff at all levels are aware of the organisation's objectives, goals, missions and successes. Then whoever speaks to a journalist gives a cohesive, coherent company message.

Chapter summary

■ It is crucial to be prepared before you speak to the press, for two reasons: to avoid saying the wrong thing and to be sure to say the right thing.

■ What you say to a journalist is, with luck, what they will write.

■ Tell the journalist what you want your customers to know.

■ Assemble all relevant facts.

■ Convert the facts to messages.

■ Include research on your market and competitors.

■ Compile all relevant and topical issues and develop opinionated messages on each.

- Have your messages reduced to short, snappy quotes and memorise them.
- Use cue cards and crib sheets.
- Anticipate predictable questions that journalists will ask and prepare your responses.
- Change the messages as the product ages.
- Prepare prepare prepare.
- Rehearse rehearse rehearse.

Case Studies

Susannah Moore	Senior PR account manager, aged 28
Company	CommunicationsLimited.com, a multi-national PR and marketing agency with 500 employees at eight offices in Europe and the US.
Clients	Mainly IT and business. Susannah is responsible for four clients, and has a junior assistant.
Target sector	IT and telecoms trade and user press.
Objective	To raise awareness of all her clients among prospective customers, board-level directors and industry analysts.
Action	Delegated the maintenance of journalist and publications database to her junior.
	Developed media strategies for each client. For two clients, arranged a joint press reception – their target journalists and publications have 90 per cent crossover. Decided to invite a local celebrity as an incentive and attraction. Unfortunately, the only one available had a reputation for being outrageous.
	Arranged one-to-one visits to publishing houses for another client. They do not have a newsworthy story at the moment, but a new product due for launch in three months' time will need preparation so that editorial coincides with the launch.
Result	Unfortunately, Susannah did not brief her junior on how to update the database or how to speak to journalists.
	Response to faxes was 100 per cent failure, and when the junior tried to telephone, most journalists were curt with her.

Susannah had to duplicate the effort to ensure that the list was accurate, but it was better than making mistakes in contact. Then she coached the junior in how to call and speak to journalists, using the right business-like tone, straight to the point and without being too familiar or 'salary'. The response rate improved immediately.

The press reception was great fun although the celebrity lived up to their reputation and created chaos. Unfortunately, neither client would do media training before the event and consequently did not understand the need not to 'sell' to the journalists. There was tongue-in-cheek 'back-page' publicity about the event, which the clients didn't appreciate and regarded as damaging. Susannah was blamed.

Recommendations   Despite the clients ignoring Susannah's advice to take media training, they blamed her for the negative publicity about the reception.

However, many journalists later remembered the clients and contacted Susannah when they were writing stories which the clients could comment on. The clients were persuaded that long-term success was as valuable and important as short-term editorial results.

Susannah now recommends that media training is compulsory for all new clients and clients' managers in press-facing roles.

Kate Banks   **News journalist, aged 26**

Description   Kate works as part of a big team on a national newspaper. This is her second job in journalism. She reports to the assistant news editor, who reports to the news editor, who reports to the deputy, who reports to the editor. She has to write three stories a day and help others on the team in their research.

Task

On Tuesdays, Kate has to write three stories for the lifestyle sidebar (short stories down the side of the page). She starts by going through the day's mail and electronic press releases.

Experience

Kate finds five press releases with possible stories. She contacts the PR at the end of the releases and finds out more. Only four are possibles – the PR for the fifth says it was used in another broadsheet the previous week.

Kate contacts the spokespeople in each release by telephone. Two are willing to talk, making time in their day to allow her to interview them immediately. The third requests an email interview, which Kate is happy to do. She outlines the points she wants to cover and the executive emails a brain-dump back to her, which Kate puts into the format she wants for the piece, selecting the parts she wants to use.

By mid-afternoon she has all her research and settles down to write her stories. She finishes the last one at 6pm.

Recommendations

Kate has obviously learned to use PRs as a resource. She is flexible and adaptable, and works with PRs to achieve an end result which suits both of them. However, to retain her professionalism and independence, she will not get too 'cosy' with any particular PRs, and will treat those who attempt to get too cosy with her with contempt.

PRs wanting to work effectively with Kate must retain their professionalism and react promptly to her wishes and requests. She will respect those who are competent, but not bother again with those who try to 'sell' her hyperbole or puff, or make promises that they fail to keep.

An efficient and professional journalist, Kate expects PRs to be the same.

5

chapter

Making contact

Introduction

Now you know about:

- the different sorts of journalists (freelance, staff, news writers and features writers)
- how to ensure that your story has at least some of the key elements which should catch their attention
- how to prepare your message so that what you tell the journalist is what you want to see appear in the media, and what you want your customers to read.

Now comes the most tricky part – actually making contact.

** Making a cold call to a busy journalist is the most terrifying thing that a PR or marketing person has to do. **

Most journalists are very busy and have no patience with time wasters. The best ones are notoriously difficult to contact and interest in a story.

<< Many PR people deserve all they get – they are creepy and sycophantic and their calls are enough to make anyone short-tempered. >>

Even junior staff journalists can be arrogant and intimidating, and, because they are busy and under pressure can be brusque to the point of rudeness. However, journalists are also looking for fresh stories, ideas, comments and opinions. If you can make contact in the right way and your story has the right hooks, the journalist *will* be interested.

Basic guidelines

Start with your database of journalists and historical notes on each. All good agencies, marketing departments and PR professionals have comprehensive details on every journalist and publication. Begin with some homework so that you know each journalist's:

■ preferred mode of initial contact

■ best days for contact

■ press days, to be avoided

■ topics, angles and issues which interest them most

■ target readers

■ preferred hospitality (breakfast, lunch, after work)

■ preferred locations

■ personal background: marital status, hobbies, interests

- career history
- history of positive or negative reporting.

You should also know whether they are staff or freelance, and the publication that they are writing for:

- the target reader, and their needs and interests
- how the publication is divided
- who does what on each section
- the deadlines of each section
- the requirements for each section
- the lead times between commission and delivery of copy.

✳✳ Put yourself in the journalist's place. You are busy, you have several deadlines looming, and you get a call from some idiot wanting to interest you in a new dishwasher or modem. It's hardly surprising that you give them short shrift. Then you've got to go back to your keyboard, and your train of thought has been broken. Of course you want to hear about new products that interest your readers, and you usually try to be patient, but after a half dozen time-wasting calls in one morning, your patience unsurprisingly runs thin. ✳✳

Do not contact the journalist on the spur of the moment.

- Do your research on the target journalist.
- Think through your story and message.
- Work out what you are going to say beforehand.
- Find out the deadlines that the journalist is likely to be working towards.

Then:

- anticipate what the journalist might say
- prepare and rehearse your responses

- have your key facts and the hook of the story written down in front of you
- have the key messages written down in front of you.

> ** Do not think that the journalist is sitting at their desk waiting to hear from you. They will be busy and you will have to sell the story to them fast, with the most interesting thing first. **

◄◄ Do not just arrive at a journalist's office without telephoning first. ►►

Know when is the best point to contact each journalist:

- on a daily – between 10 and 2
- on a weekly – Tuesday for a Sunday, Sunday for a Monday, Friday for a Tuesday.

Don't call them:

- after 4.30 on a daily
- or Friday afternoon for a Sunday or Monday
- just before a copy deadline
- before 10 or 10.30am.

Who should you call?

In Chapter One we looked at the different types of journalist and the different job titles on each publication or programme. Create a list of those which are most likely to be interested in your story.

Don't just contact one journalist for each publication. Speak to as many on each title as are appropriate for your story. Tailor your opening sentence to the publication's reader, then to the particular journalist. Prepare and rehearse, prepare and rehearse.

✳✳ Many freelances work only to commission and don't have to 'sell' a story to an editor. Others do, and need to constantly pitch ideas to the commissioning editors. Part of your research should determine how each publication and journalist works. ✳✳

If you already know a journalist on a publication, contact them first. Even if they are not interested they may know who you should talk to.

≪ Any initiative to interest a publication in a story should be made to at least two levels – senior and junior. It is the senior staff who decide what goes in, but the junior staff who write it. ≫

Ultimately, it is the editor who decides what goes into the publication or programme, although they often discuss it with the section heads (news editors, features editors). The actual writing will probably be done by staff journalists or freelances.

> ✳✳ If the editors don't know about your story, when they see it in the copy they won't appreciate its importance and might even remove it. If the staffers and freelances don't know about your story, they won't be able to include it. Don't rely on the editor to instruct the writers to include it – you must make sure that they *all* know about it. ✳✳

The process on many magazines and newspapers is as follows:

- The editor is often the first to see the press release or to receive the pitch phone call.
- They instruct the staff or freelance journalist to follow up the story.
- Sometimes journalists get the news first and 'sells' it to the editor.
- Sometimes the editorial assistant opens all the post addressed to the title and creates a pile of releases which is circulated to everyone.

- Sometimes staff journalists are free to follow stories which they think are most important.
- Some freelances have to 'sell' stories to the commissioning editor.
- The final decision about whether to include the story ultimately always rests with the editor.
- In radio and TV the editors and reporters often work together to decide which story to follow up.
- Once the journalist has written the piece and the reporter has prepared their report, the sub-editor or editor then proofreads it and checks it.
- The sub will make sure that it:
  - appeals to the target reader, viewer or listener
  - is timely
  - is newsworthy
  - is not libellous or inaccurate
  - is fair, with the right balance of views
  - is in good taste.

Some journalists:

- like to receive unsolicited case studies
- want every press release
- like to get photographs
- like to get demo or sample software
- like to get review copies of books
- dislike all those and sling everything straight in the bin.

Follow up each contact with a journalist by sending a picture of a person and the product to the sub-editor, with a note on the back saying:

- who it is
- their job title
- company name

- company switchboard number
- web site address
- which story it is to go with.

◄◄ Some publications are driven by the pictures that they have. If they get a particularly good photograph, they can choose the story that goes with it. ►►

How should you make contact?

There are several traditional ways to contact journalists, each with their own advantages and disadvantages. Remember though, each journalist will have their own preferred way: find out what that is by asking them, then stick to that preferred mode. This might be:

- email
- telephone
- snail-mail post
- voicemail
- fax
- personal visit.

◄◄ Remember that the journalist might get hundreds of press releases each week and dozens of phone calls each day, plus many emails. Its hardly surprising that junior staff journalists can become arrogant and rude when they are being courted from all sides by PRs wanting to tell them about their product, take them out to lunch, take them on trips, etc. Naturally it goes to their head and they think they are so popular. ►►

** You have to play the game by the journalists' rules. Just because you think it is cheaper to send press releases by email, if the journalist prefers snail mail that's the way you have to do it. **

✳✳ Each journalist might have a different preference for different reasons for the contact ... for example, they might prefer email for press releases but telephone for invitations, or snail-mail post for invitations and press releases but email for anything else. Keep your list accurate by asking each journalist which they prefer. ✳✳

See Appendix 3 on how to write an effective press release.

Email

This is undoubtedly the easiest way for both PRs and journalists for first contact.

Positive	Negative
Relatively pain-free for the PR	Lacks the personal touch
The journalist can respond at their leisure	The journalist might not respond at all
Can be a good way to maintain a relationship without extensive time and effort	Some journalists hate emailed press releases – they have to print them out or keep them on disk
A personal relationship can develop which can pay big dividends in the future	
Cheap	

There is an art to writing successful emails.

▓ Keep it as short as possible.

▓ Don't be too familiar – err on the side of formality.

▓ If you use a long list of recipients and copy them all in on one message, make sure that the list is hidden and each journalist thinks it is aimed at them personally.

- Put a summary of the email in the first sentence – preferably the hook for the reader.

- Don't send large attachments, at least without asking the journalist first.

- If you are sending an invitation by email, give all the details including who will be there, and the value the journalist is likely to derive from attending.

- Put all your contact details, including post and telephone, at the end.

- If you plan to telephone later, say so in the email.

- Ask the journalist to email back an acknowledgement and to say whether the story might be of interest. They may not all respond, but some might.

Telephone

Depending on the response to your email, you can follow up with a telephone call – the most feared and terrifying challenge to anyone trying to promote a product. At least by emailing first, you avoid that dreaded first 'cold-contact' telephone call.

** You must have exactly the right approach or the journalist will be rude or curt. **

Positive	Negative
You get straight through – very direct	You risk rudeness and refusal
You will know the journalist's reaction immediately	Once they've turned you down, it is harder to try again by this or any other method
Can do more to develop the relationship than email or post	Some journalists hate the telephone and regard calls from PRs as an intrusion
Some journalists insist on a telephone call as the first contact	Time consuming

Snail-mail post

Emails should also be followed up with snail-mail letters.

Outline the point of your email and include press releases, case studies, anything else that is relevant.

Positive	Negative
You have the time to outline your story	Might go straight into the bin
Personally targeted – can take an individual approach for each journalist	You have no way of knowing the reaction
	Not as fast as email or telephone
Gets your brand and logo across the journalist's desk	
Some journalists prefer all press releases by snail-mail post – it is easier to open an envelope than print out an email	

- Get all the important points across in the first paragraph.
- Enclose a photograph, particularly to journalists working on publications.
- Think twice about sending expensive photographs to freelances unless they request them.
- Make sure your mailing list is up to date and regularly cleaned.

Voicemail

There is also an art to leaving a good voicemail.

- Keep it short.
- Speak clearly.
- Give your name and company name.

- Repeat the phone number.

- Give your email address as an option.

- If your call is not returned, call the journalist again or email them – many journalists never return voicemail messages on the principle that if it is important the person will call back.

- Never leave a long and complicated message, just your name and a return phone number, and a brief indication of the purpose of your call.

- Check your messages regularly, in case the journalist has called you back.

Fax

Though these are increasingly outdated, many journalists still have fax machines and some PRs like to use them.

- Like e-mails, faxes should be as short as possible.

- Don't send a fax unless you are sure that the journalist wants it.

** Faxes are dead. They clutter up the journalist's desk with yards of curling paper. Only use when essential, and usually only when requested by the journalist. **

Visit

- If the journalist is expecting you, a quick personal visit to explain the story or pitch can be highly effective for both short and long-term editorial.

- Never visit a journalist without calling first.

- Many journalists appreciate being taken out for a drink after work or a quick lunch.

- Make the purpose of the meeting as much to develop the relationship as to tell your story.

- Keep it informal.

** The most difficult way to contact journalists, and the highest failure rate, is by telephone. Cute mailers are a waste of time, and email can be ignored. Fax is old fashioned. You could resort to accidentally bumping into them in Sainsbury's. **

The pitch

You will need to pitch stories to:

- freelances in the hope that they in turn will sell the idea to commissioning editors
- staffers in the hope that they will sell the idea to their editor or section editor
- the editors and section editors in the hope that they will commission a writer to do the story.

When you call to pitch an idea for a story:

- you must be convincing. Unless you believe it, the journalist certainly won't – the sizzle is as interesting as the steak
- you must know the product and company
- you must be prepared for the journalist to ask questions
- they are unlikely to take the story exactly as you pitch it to them
- they will try to find their own angle
- they will want to talk to your competitors as well.

** There is nothing much more irritating for a journalist than to be contacted by someone trying to pitch something that they don't understand, who is obviously reading from a script, and who doesn't understand the readers or know the publication either. No wonder journalists are so intolerant of PR people – so many of them are incompetent amateurs. **

There are other factors to bear in mind.

- Journalists are expecting to receive suggestions from people like you with a vested interest. They get them all the time.

- Declare your interest from the outset.

- Do not attempt to mislead the journalist into thinking that you are independent.

- They will be critical of the story's validity, and sceptical.

- Be prepared for them to want to talk to users, your competitors, independent analysts and specialist pundits.

- Be aware of their deadlines before you call – if you don't know them, ask.

- When you call, have their target audience in mind.

- Have your crib sheet to hand, outlining your key messages and the main features of the product, and its implications for the audience.

- Don't waste a journalist's time. Never call without something specific to say.

- Get straight to the point without overly courteous preambles.

- Journalists are usually willing to listen to most stories in the hope that they will find something that will interest their listeners, viewers or readers – you have about 30 seconds to get their interest.

- They need you because they are continually looking for good new stories.

- They will give you a chance, but you must come straight to the point.

- Don't waste their time or expect flowery pleasantries about the weather.

- If the journalist is brusque, don't take it personally.

- Be business-like and don't over-sell.

- A successful pitch is explicit about the interest of the audience in the story. A pitch which is just a basic 'We've launched a new product' invites the response 'So what?'.

- The journalist is bound to take a view opposing whatever you are saying – that is what they are supposed to do. Don't take their cynicism personally.

Start with your name and company, then ask:

- 'Is this a good time to call?'
- 'Do you have two minutes to talk to me, please?'

Don't just launch into your pitch.

- Say 'I'll just take two or three minutes of your time to suggest a story to you', then quickly run through the idea.
- Have a press release ready to send the moment you put the phone down after pitching.
- As the pitch proceeds, listen to what the journalist is saying.
- Stop halfway through and say, 'Is this interesting for you?'
- If the journalist asks questions, respond with appropriate answers.
- Be led by the journalist's line of questions.

Successful pitches are well organised and prepared.

- There is a basic structure.
- The interest and relevance to the audience are clearly apparent.
- The language is simple and direct.

Unsuccessful pitches may be:

- badly timed
- without any obvious point or relevance to the journalist's customer
- too familiar
- too full of jargon.

** Whatever you do, avoid jargon unless you know the journalist well. **

Words that you use all the time may be utterly impenetrable to someone outside your area of expertise. It can be very hard to eliminate all jargon, but it is essential to try – focus on the benefits rather than the technology.

Journalists think that people who use jargon:

- are insecure
- are showing off that they belong to an esoteric world
- use too many words to say too little
- are not in touch with their readers.

Instead, translate technical or trade-speak to consumer-speak by replacing abbreviations, acronyms and unnecessarily complex words or phrases with simple ones.

> ** Many firms and organisations have an internal jargon which is impossible for an outsider to decode. It is easy to get into the habit of using complex words to describe simple ideas or features. Techno-speak, marketing-speak and company-speak should all be avoided. **

- Keep your communications simple and unfussy and the journalist is more likely to listen to what you have to say.
- If a journalist is unable to understand, they will not necessarily ask you to slow, stop or repeat yourself.
- Journalists, particularly novices, will sometimes pretend they understand when they don't.
- Speak and write in clear, jargon-free terms.
- Avoid clichés – those vivid verbal phrases which are amusing or appropriate the first time will quickly pall like a bad joke.

Pegs, hooks and angles

Every story must have a 'hook' – the most interesting angle relevant to the journalist and their customer. It is what the journalist will use to interest their reader, viewer or listener.

** Don't be afraid to point out the hook to the journalist, even if it is obvious to you. **

◀◀ The hook or angle is always of interest or benefit to the reader. ▶▶

The journalist might see a hook that you missed or didn't want to see – you have to follow the journalist's line of interest.

** Some of the best stories are those which some people don't want printed, and journalists will always be looking for an angle which you may not want them to follow. Tough. **

Offering exclusives

Some inexperienced PRs believe that if they give a key journalist a story on the basis that it is an exclusive they are more likely to use it.

But:

- you have no control over whether they will use it – having an exclusive will not replace any lack of hook
- once you give it to one, the rest won't want it because by then it will be old news
- some journalists accept 'exclusives' and then do not use the story, as a spoiler to their competitors – there is nothing you can do
- you have no control over what they write about, and even if they write the story, it may later be spiked by the editor.

** If the story is a good, strong one, you will not need to offer it to any journalist as an exclusive – they will all want it anyway. **

Gifts and freebies

There is always a chance that gifts might be perceived as a gauche attempt at a bribe, but they can also be excellent ways to improve journalists' attitude and awareness of a company or product. Gifts and freebies vary from the ubiquitous mouse mat (how many can one person use?) to expensive corporate gifts, hampers, booze, etc. Generally, the Brits are renowned for not refusing free gifts, however small, and journalists are, generally speaking, no exception.

** If you think that by giving a gift the journalist will favour you with positive editorial coverage, you are living in a dream. Sometimes the reverse is even true – they demonstrate that they cannot be bought by ignoring you. But most journalists still like gifts and free products. The trick is to give the gift without any expectation … when you do that, you are pleased with whatever results. **

Positive	Negative
Good for the relationship	The journalist might take the gift and then deliberately avoid mentioning you to show that they cannot be 'bought'
Good for raising awareness/as an *aide mémoire* of your product and brand.	
Can help considerably by making sure the journalist remembers you and the brand	Can backfire with column inches devoted to the idiocy of gifts and freebies
Useful to maintain awareness of you or your product brand	

- It's not a bribe unless it's a secret.
- Send a press release or letter about your company and product along with the gift.
- All gifts should be given without any expectations and with no strings attached.

- Don't waste your budget by sending an inappropriate gift to a journalist who is never going to use it. Be selective.

- In the UK, few journalists turn down the offer of a gift or a freebie provided they come without strings.

- UK journalists rarely refuse gifts and freebies on the grounds that they might compromise their independence and integrity. At Christmas in particular many journalists receive corporate gifts such as port and Stilton, wine and other giveaways. These are usually gratefully received, without any feeling of obligation to favour the provider in the new year.

- Most journalists are grateful for gifts, tickets for corporate hospitality events, etc. at any time of the year, but there needs to be the strict understanding that they are given and received without any expectation of editorial publicity.

- In America the situation is quite different. It is a sackable offence on many US titles for their journalists to accept freebies. Most US publishing houses give their journalists an expense account so that they can pay for their own meals and travel to events and meetings without relying on the hospitality of a PR company or someone seeking to promote their product. Some UK titles take a similar view, although they are in the minority. Few UK journalists have a budget for expenses.

- As with hospitality, if you are unsure of the protocol with particular titles or individual journalists, ask.

Stunts and teasers

PR professionals take different views of stunts (gimmicks to catch the journalists' attention) and teasers (vague announcements that something is coming soon in the hope of intriguing the journalist).

** If you have a story to tell a journalist, just get on with it and tell them – don't faff around trying to make a meal out of it. **

Positive	Negative
Can intrigue and catch the journalists' attention	Can misfire badly and create unexpected negative press
Can grab more attention than a press release	Can have no reaction at all
Can create interaction between the organisers and the media	Hard to find ones which have not been done before
Can create excellent photo opportunities	Journalists often dislike them
Can appeal to a wide range of journalists and media	Many journalists find them irritating
	Highly risky and vulnerable to problems
Some journalists love them	Can be costly to arrange

◀◀ Keeping something back from journalists in the hope of intriguing them can alienate them. ▶▶

There are various types of teaser campaign.

- A series of press release mailings in advance of the true release, which are supposed to whet journalists' appetite for a story.
- A series of small, anonymous gifts which lead up to and culminate in the full story.

However:

- if the product or story is interesting it won't need tricks to catch the journalists' eye
- if your product or story is dull and you are having trouble finding a hook, then a stunt may be the only way of catching the journalists' eye
- once the press realises that the product is dull and there is no good hook, they will reject the story anyway, regardless of the stunt or teaser.

> << The secret is to know your journalists, and know which might be receptive to a stunt or teaser and which will be annoyed by them. >>

Dealing with attitude

Most journalists are perfectly nice and charming and polite to PRs. However, some key journalists are notoriously difficult, rude and arrogant. This might not be their natural personality but because they are trying to be independent and critical.

- Do not confuse professional cynicism with rudeness. The journalist will try to ask all the questions which their viewers and readers might like to ask.

- The journalist will attempt to strip away hype and cant.

- It is not your job to try to 'teach the journalist a lesson'.

- You have to continue to be polite and professional.

- Do not be rebuffed immediately. Try to develop the relationship in other ways, such as offering hospitality.

- If there is clearly a natural antipathy (no one likes everyone), find another key journalist to approach.

** PR is a contact sport and it has to be played like that – it can be tough and sometimes you can get hurt. **

Responding to features lists

** Don't submit long features written in house or commissioned from a journalist by you, without discussing it with the features editor first. **

Imagine – a list of features from each magazine, newspaper and programme which gives you every feature they are planning for the next year, with subject, angle, the journalist commissioned to write it and the deadline. What could be easier, you might think, to be sure that you get your product or company mentioned. Sorry, features lists can be useful, but:

- they are subject to change – they are often written a year in advance and key topics change
- the deadlines given may have passed by the time you get the list
- features may be held over even after they have been written and delivered.

** Features lists are created by the editorial team for the media sales teams to sell against. They are not aimed at PRs to help them get editorial coverage. **

Respond by:

- contacting the journalist immediately. The deadline will be their deadline to deliver, and they will be looking for input long before that
- delivering interesting and opinionated views, not boring sales information. Then you stand a good chance of being mentioned.

◀◀ Contact the media sales team of each key publication and ask for their forward features list. Some editorial teams also distribute them to PRs and marketing professionals. ▶▶

Some editors refuse to produce features lists, claiming that they compromise editorial integrity and independence. Those titles which have no influence from the sale; team have more controversial, independent and less sycophantic editorial than those with close links between advertising and editorial than are more inclined to quote advertisers in their copy.

After you speak to a journalist you may get a call from the advertising team trying to sell you advertising. Sometimes the sales executive will insinuate that unless you advertise in the publication, your editorial mention will be dropped. In fact, this is rarely the case and there is no reason for you to advertise just because you are mentioned in the editorial.

On the other hand if you place an advertisement because of a feature on a particular topic, ask whether you can speak to a journalist. On some titles, particularly smaller trade ones, the journalists are under pressure to talk to advertisers and will try to mention advertisers positively in the editorial. The safest way to leverage your advertising is through the advertising team, not by going direct to the journalist. (See Chapter Three on the relationship between advertising and editorial.)

> ✱✱ PRs should respond to news and features stories that appear in the media. Many publications are happy or keen to keep a story running with subsequent comments and views. Contact the publication as soon as you read, see or hear anything you think you should have been included in or have a comment to make on. You may extend the debate. ✱✱

There are several electronic versions of features list, including Sourcewire (*www.sourcewire.com*) which journalists use to request information from PR companies. See Appendix 3 for other similar services, where PRs can find out which features are being planned by specific publications.

Deadlines

All publications and programmes have deadlines, and it is important to know what they are. The quickest way to find out is to ask the editorial team.

- A single publication can have several deadlines – the ones that should concern you are those for the journalists to deliver copy.
- A deadline is not the cut-off for you to deliver information. It is the final time for the journalist to finish the piece and deliver it.
- The journalist may need input days or weeks before their deadline to deliver copy.

- Because of their other commitments, the journalist may write their copy well before the deadline.
- Deadlines can be false to make sure that copy is received in time.

Your rule of thumb: set your own deadline several hours or days earlier.

> ** Deal with journalists' requests immediately – don't assume that because the deadline is several days or weeks away that you don't need to respond at once. **

Deadlines are connected to the frequency of the publication.

- Internet titles are updated almost continually and have running deadlines.
- Dailies may work on tomorrow's news today, working on the fastest-moving stories right up to the deadline but finishing less time-sensitive features earlier. At most they have a two-day lead time. Deadlines on dailies are sometimes hourly and news comes in right up to the moment the issue closes. Dailies also have features which have longer deadlines. News stories are sometimes carried over, but the story is usually too dated by the next day. Features may be held over for a week or more. Local radio is often looking for stories each morning.
- Weeklies are often divided into news, which has a weekly deadline, and features, which has deadlines a couple of weeks before publication.
- Monthlies often have features written two months before they close, which is often three months before the publication appears. There is often a two or three-week 'dead time' between closing and appearing because they are printed cheaply, in sections, between other more important jobs. Monthlies rarely have topical news, preferring instead to run news analysis.

** If you fail to respond before the deadline the journalist will not wait. A deadline is just that – a cut-off point. They cannot be held up or changed easily. **

≪ Once a journalist has enough comment or fact they will not want to keep talking to other people – you not only have to beat the deadline, you have to beat others also trying to get editorial coverage. And it is very competitive. ≫

Journalists work against tight deadlines all the time. Deadlines:

- generate a sense of urgency which produces an intense and creative atmosphere
- encourage interviewees to comment spontaneously.

✻✻ Some journalists claim that they are working against a tight deadline to get an unrehearsed and off-the-cuff statement which can make good copy. They will say that their deadline is tight when in fact it is not – it's one of the journalist's oldest tricks. ✻✻

Whatever the real deadline, if the journalist says their deadline is two hours, two days or two weeks away, you have to accept that. Aim to deliver your information or comments as soon as possible, not as close to the deadline as possible. You may have a great story, but deliver it at the wrong time and it will not be used.

≪ If you don't respond fast and meet the journalist's deadline, there are plenty of other people who will and you will miss an editorial opportunity. ≫

If you are unable to respond to a specific request by a journalist in time, give the journalist a courtesy call or email to tell them.

What happens to the information or comments you provide?

If your information or comments are:

- not relevant for that particular journalist or audience
- old news

- received after the deadline
- not eye-catching
- too obscure

or

- there were other stories more interesting or relevant
- the journalist already has enough comments or information

your posted comments, press release and emailed material will

- end up in the bin
- or be held over until another feature or issue
- be used several times in various features and news stories.

** Giving information to journalists is a lottery which relies on factors outside your control. You have no control over the mood of the editor, other stories coming in or events taking place, or your competitors' activities. **

Maintaining the long-term relationship

Media relations is all about personal relationships between individual PR and marketing professionals and individual journalists. It is far easier for you to make contact with a journalist with whom you already have a relationship, so try to cement and build relationships whenever you can.

Get to know your key journalists whenever you can.

- Email or telephone and ask which is their preferred method of receiving information.
- Ask how they like to receive press releases.
- Ask whether they would like to go out for a drink or have a meal (with or without a client).

- Find out what each journalist is interested in and what they are looking for in a story by asking them.

- Once you have made contact through a press reception or event, or by contact over a specific feature, keep the relationship going (see Chapter Eight on following up).

Once you have a contact, maintain an honest, open and friendly relationship, but remember that very few journalists actually *like* PR people – they have different agendas, and are frequently different sorts of people. But like cats and dogs they can often rub along amicably to their mutual advantage. The PR person has the budget for entertaining and the journalist has the direct and persuasive route to the customers – there is mutual advantage in a trusting relationship.

** Few journalists mind when PRs call to find how they prefer to receive information or to ask them out for a drink. **

> << Journalists don't usually mind regular calls to 'see if you are working on anything that we can help you with'. If they do mind, don't call them with that question again. >>

So, it's not working ...

If despite repeated efforts the journalist is not responding and plainly not interested in you or your product or story, ask yourself: what are you doing wrong?

We know that:

- journalists are continually looking for stories
- they are running stories from your competitors

so if you are not getting editorial coverage after months of pitching, press release and meetings, you are obviously doing something wrong.

It may be:

- that your pitches are not relevant
- you irritate the journalist
- you have not done enough research
- your story does not have an appropriate hook.

Sometimes a fresh face changes everything – pass contact with that particular journalist to a colleague or an outside agency.

** You are always at the mercy of the journalist's personal preferences. **

** If you don't like the journalist, the feeling is probably mutual. **

No professional journalist would ignore a story because they don't like the person pitching it, but mutual antipathy doesn't help. Don't take it personally – you can't win 'em all.

<< There is no guaranteed method of assuring editorial coverage – you just have to do your best and then hope. >>

Chapter summary

- Successful contact with journalists depends hugely on the quality of your background research.
- Be selective about the titles and journalists you target.
- Use your database of publications and programmes detailing copy deadlines, special columns, feature sections, whether they use case studies and opinion pieces, etc.
- Keep your database updated.

- Read the publications/watch the programmes of the journalists you contact.

- Use email first, follow up with telephone and post.

- Fax is dated.

- Be prepared before you call – have a script.

- Think about what the journalist might say.

- Don't call on press day.

- The journalist will want to hear from you, but not if you have nothing to say.

- Don't ramble or use unnecessary pleasantries. Don't even ask 'How are you?' unless you mean it. Get straight to the point and be business-like.

- Listen to what the journalist says and respond to them.

- Make sure there is a clear hook to the story which is relevant to the journalist's audience.

- If the journalist is offhand or rude, don't take it personally.

- If you are really not connecting with a journalist and you feel hostility, don't exacerbate the situation by persevering.

- If you make a good contact, develop the relationship.

Case studies

Eddie Newman	Self-employed PR consultant, aged 35
Company	Runs OneStopPR, a one-man PR service for six long-standing clients.
Clients	Three IT firms, a business consultancy and two retail chains. Eddie has a team of three working for him and has been in PR for 15 years.
Target sector	National and specialist business and consumer press.
Objective	To raise awareness of all his clients among prospective customers, both business and consumer, and industry analysts.
Action	Eddie has detailed campaigns for each client, but wants to achieve an economy of scale by running a joint event. He organised a combined press reception for all six clients and arranged for a total of 40 client executives to meet invited journalists.
Result	Unfortunately, the date Eddie chose turned out to be the day that the transport system went on strike. From an original invitation list of 150, there were 60 definite acceptances. Five managed to make it.
	Luckily many of his clients' executives were also unable to get to the venue, so he had only 15 to entertain. Still, the 20 journalists and clients, plus his own PR staff, had a good time and got to know each other very well by the end of the evening.
	Fortunately, the outcome was very positive – PRs, clients and journalists united by an external conspiracy to disrupt. After the evening, the clients were very satisfied. Several journalists requested further information about products, and coverage for the clients improved over the next six months.

Recommendations   There is little that Eddie could have done to anticipate the situation. As it was, the turnout was just enough to be credible – he has known events that were not victim to the unexpected generating less turnout.

Sam White	Editor, aged 37

Description   Sam has been a journalist for ten years after passing his accountancy exams. He chose not to practice, but now writes about accounting issues and the accounting world for the leading magazine for the profession.

Sam manages a team of five journalists, two sub-editors and a production editor, and a designer. He uses very few freelances because the work is detailed and requires qualified understanding of accountancy. He only has time to write the editor's foreword and one feature each month – the rest of his time is spent commissioning, planning, managing his team and in meetings with the publisher and sales teams.

Task   It is press day, and Sam has to pass pages. He has also accepted three invitations to briefings and seminars, and wants to meet the newly appointed finance director of a large American conglomerate who is in town for one day only.

Experience   Sam has to prioritise and the magazine is most important. He delegates some of the proofreading to one of his subs, but as both subs worked on the original copy that is not satisfactory. He ropes in one of the journalists to help read through page proofs. Sam creates enough time to attend a lunchtime seminar, where he meets senior analysts from a major research firm, but he doesn't turn up for any of the other events. He doesn't call to say he won't be attending after all. He calls a freelance who is attending one to request a news story if it is worth reporting on.

He is not able to meet the FD, but arranges a video conference with him the following week, when the FD is back in the States.

Recommendations   Ideally Sam should have an assistant helping him to plan his time. Editorial work always takes precedence over meetings, but often seminars and briefings are good sources of news stories and features ideas, although not on press day. Another time, the disappointed PRs will ensure that their events don't coincide with press day.

The interview

Introduction

You have your messages, so why is it necessary to give an interview too? Because research shows that only 20 per cent of editorial content comes from prepared messages while 30 per cent comes from unexpected ad hoc comments. Another 10 per cent comes from non-verbal communications, i.e. the way you look or sound.

Interviews are your chance to persuade a journalist with your arguments, impress them with your knowledge and amuse them with your wit. If you don't have arguments and don't feel witty or able to think on your feet, *you should still give every interview you can*.

◀◀The journalist usually wants information, comments, views and opinions – they are not setting out to trap or trick you. Try to relax and treat the 'interview' like a conversation and you'll be fine.▶▶

✳✳The journalist is talking to you because you are the expert on the subject. ✳✳

Why do an interview?

Interviews are:

- an opportunity to promote your product, brand and company
- an opportunity to increase customer awareness and therefore profits.

✳✳Your problem is that you are playing the journalist's game, in their territory, using their rules. ✳✳

If you understand something about the rules they use and the agenda they are working from, you can turn the opportunity to your advantage. If you don't take advantage of an opportunity to talk to the media, your competitors surely will.

✳✳People get very worked up over interviews, but most journalists are just looking for information and opinion, and they are all looking for good copy for their readers. That's it. It's not the grilling that many people imagine it is going to be. ✳✳

Interviews often feel just like a chat, but don't be lulled into a false sense of security: the journalist is free to print or broadcast anything you say.

✳✳Journalists are always on duty. ✳✳

So don't necessarily get too frank but do get opinionated and assertive.

The journalist will be far more experienced at interviewing than you, but you are the expert on the issue or topic, that's why they are talking to you.

If you are nervous, try not to let it show. The journalist:

■ will think that you are trying to hide something

■ may try to dig even deeper.

On the other hand, journalists are not completely unfeeling and they are unlikely to bully those who are obviously nervous. They are more likely to be tough on those who appear arrogant, pompous and cocky.

✱✱ Most inaccuracies in the press are there because PRs are incompetent. **✱✱**

✱✱Journalists are like jackdaws – they pick up a little bit of information here and there. But they rarely know a complex subject in great depth, they know a little about a lot of things. So you are almost sure to know more than they do. That's why they want to talk to you. **✱✱**

Should you ever refuse an interview?

If you feel nervous or your client is obviously unprepared, you might ask 'Should we do this interview?' If you are trying to promote your product, the answer is usually 'Yes'!

✱✱There are plenty of other PRs and companies eager for the opportunity. If you pass it up, others will be keen to take your place, including your competitors. **✱✱**

It would be a waste of an opportunity to refuse an interview if:

■ a journalist calls you as the result of a press release

■ you already know the journalist

■ a journalist is writing on a topic which is close to your core business.

However, it makes sense to stall an interview, if only for half an hour, if you want to:

■ check your facts

■ find out more about the journalist and their publication

- get some background material in front of you
- go through your messages
- get someone else in on the interview.

You can always refuse to do an interview if you think that:

- the journalist is going to be hostile
- they want comment on bad news, and it is not your job responsibility
- there is someone better prepared or more knowledgeable than you
- you really don't think you have anything worthwhile to say
- you believe you may emerge battered
- you think your competitors may do better and your image will suffer
- you will not get a chance to say what you want.

** Refusing to be interviewed can look like you have something to hide. **

If you really believe it is best to refuse:

- be polite – don't just hang up or say 'No comment'
- give a credible reason
- offer to be interviewed another time
- make it clear that your refusal to be interviewed is not company policy
- suggest other topics that you would be delighted to comment on
- say something like this, 'I'd love to be able to comment on that but unfortunately I'm not the right person in this instance/I'm about to go into a meeting. However, if there is anything else I can help you with/anything else you want to talk about/I can talk to you tomorrow/next week, please tell me or get back to me.'

The worst outcome is either 'we asked the company to comment but they declined' or 'No comment'. Both are highly damning and suggest you have something to hide.

Sometimes PR people act like a gatekeeper between the journalist and their client or the senior manager, and actually stop the free flowing of information and comments. They always want to be involved. It's usually better if they make the introduction and then let the journalist contact their client or the pundit manager whenever they want to, direct.

Preparing for an interview

Be prepared. If you think that a journalist might telephone unexpectedly, or you are expecting an interview, prepare a one-page check list to ensure that you maintain control of the interview and get all the information you need. This form will act as:

- an *aide mémoire* when you review your interviews
- a prompt for delivering follow-up information to the media.

Use a form every time you speak to a journalist.

- Have hard copies on the desk of every executive or manager who might talk to the media.
- Have electronic versions on your PDA (personal digital assistant).
- Have an electronic workflow version on your PC linked to other departments, such as marketing.

In the few minutes before an interview, check back on your messages prepared in Chapter Four, consider the topic of the interview, and prepare the three key points that you really want to get across in this interview and want to see in print.

Interview check sheet/record

Your name

Your job title

Date

Name of journalist

Contact telephone number

Email

Staff or freelance?

Name of title/programme

News or feature?

DEADLINE

Topic of interview

Questions & answers

Who else have they spoken to?

What else are they working on?

Follow-up action

(photographs, press releases, user names,

reference sites, statistics, facts?)

Message check list

Topic of this interview

Date

Journalist

Journalist's contact number

Message one/Point one

Message two/Point two

Message three/Point three

The worst questions a journalist might ask

What are your responses going to be?

Topics you want to 'ring-fence' and avoid
discussing with the media

1.

2.

3.

Follow-up action

Types of interview

The interview might be:

- face to face
- by telephone
- by email.

	Positive	Negative
Face to face	Can be formal or casual	Hard to get away
	Can convey more meaning	Expensive
	Eye contact	Time consuming
	Able to be extremely responsive	More protocols and courtesies to be observed
	Can last longer	
	Able to use personality to sell the positive aspects	More difficult to make notes
		Harder to use cue cards and crib sheets
	Can deal with journalists' comments and criticisms immediately	
	Body language can be helpful	
Telephone	Direct, can be succinct and to the point	Easy to end
	Can be abrupt	No eye contact
	Can be unannounced when you are unprepared	
	Able to tailor responses to each journalist's requirements	
	Able to deal with journalists' comments immediately	
	Economic	
	Easier to use cue cards and crib sheets	

	Positive	Negative
Email	Can answer questions at your leisure	No eye contact
	Cheap	Hard to determine journalists' reactions
	Record of questions and answers	
	Easier to deliver opinions and views to a wide range and number of journalists.	

The interview might be:

- for information
- for hard news
- to get comments, views, opinions and quotes
- for research
- for confirmation
- it is unlikely to be intensely interrogative.

Or it might be:

- expected
- unexpected/impromptu
- over a meal
- at a press reception or conference
- short (no more than a couple of minutes)
- average (5–30 minutes)
- long (on a press trip, the whole time)
- friendly
- adversarial
- emotional
- entertaining.

** People listen to John Humphrys and Jeremy Paxman interviewing politicians and think every interview is going to be like that … some people are even disappointed when they are not. In fact, most interviews are tame, friendly affairs where the journalist is mainly quiet and expects the interviewee to keep talking. **

Every interview is different, but most are straightforward deliveries of information and opinion. Few are like the grilling that you see on *Newsnight* or hear on Radio 4.

The journalist's approach

** Don't expect the journalist to be friendly and don't be surprised if they seem offhand or even hostile – they are creating distance between you in an effort to remain professional and distant. If they get too friendly they will find it harder to be critical or ask difficult questions which deliver the answers and information they want for their readers. **

No two journalists are exactly the same. There are many different styles and approaches.

However, all are:

- potentially dangerous
- able to ask questions which get right to the nub of the issue
- able to get the interviewees to say something that is accurate but not what they wanted to say.

**Strange as it may seem, some journalists have a telephone phobia. They avoid the telephone and dislike doing telephone interviews. Others dislike meeting people in the flesh, preferring telephone or email. The key is to know each journalist's likes and dis-likes, and respect them. **

They may vary between these extremes.

John Humphrys	Jeremy Paxman	Sir David Frost
Interrogative, aggressive	Interrogative, aggressive	Gentle, conversational, friendly
Overtly combative	Overtly combative	Relaxed and calm
Constantly interrupts to off-balance interviewee	Sneering, dismissive, intolerant of fools	Gives interviewees an apparently easy time
Impatient, appears to bully and brow-beat	Cynical, world-weary	Aims to make the interviewee relax
Very direct	Scathing, caustic	Lulls the interviewee into a sense of security
	Dauntingly intelligent	Invites interviewees to share a confidence
		Then goes for the jugular with incisive questions
		Iron fist in a kid glove

Any good journalist will:

- prompt you
- challenge you
- say nothing, keeping quiet while you fill the silence
- be prepared
- know about all the skeletons in your cupboard
- know all about your market and competitors.

Any good interviewers will be:

- tough-minded
- sharp
- sceptical
- informed
- not partisan.

> **The BBC requires its journalists to be 'not aggressive, hectoring or rude, but tough-minded, sharp, sceptical, well informed, and not partial, committed or emotionally attached to one side of the argument'.**

The journalist will:

- ask questions on behalf of the viewer, listener or reader
- ask questions which may not reflect their own opinions or views.

> Journalists are like the little boy in the story of *The Emperor's New Clothes* – boldly asking things which others are too afraid to mention.

The journalist will be acting as a devil's advocate on behalf of their customer, their reader or viewer.

Sometimes the journalist's questions will appear naive or innocent. Don't believe that this is necessarily the case. Keep your answers equally simple.

> The journalist does not necessarily want the interviewee to appear in a bad light, but is just attempting to get the best story. They usually want you to perform well.

The journalist:

- will not let wild claims go unchallenged
- will not accept unsubstantiated assumptions
- will try to find your weakness
- will try to establish whether you are lying, exaggerating or misleading
- will not be deterred or impressed by position, money or power.

Handling the interview

There are various tactics that journalists are trained to use.

- Posing apparently simple questions which can reveal a lot more than the interviewees realise.

- Asking complex questions bolted together in rapid succession in an attempt to confuse and provoke.

- Keeping quiet – this old sales trick encourages interviewees to keep talking.

- Switching between friendly and hostile – can be disconcerting.

- Bullying-hassling – putting the interviewee under pressure.

- Claiming to be under a tight deadline – and forcing an unconsidered response.

- Being apparently misleading or disingenuous – allows you an opportunity to put them right. Failure to do so is tacit agreement.

- Making inaccurate assumptions – again, provokes response but also gives an opportunity to give the accurate facts.

- Appearing to end an interview – closing a notepad or starting to chat about something else can give the signal that the interview is over. It's never over until you are down the street, or the phone has been put down. The journalist is always working.

- Asking a sneaky last question (à la Detective Colombo) which is actually the most incisive – people are often relaxed at that point and reply without thinking.

Despite the view that journalists are all rottweilers intent on misquoting and causing trouble, few actually behave that way. Few will spring anything particularly tricky unless they know that you have been trained to deal with difficult questions or you have a public job for which you can reasonably be expected to deal with criticism from the press.

In fact, the opposite is often true. Many journalists will seek to comfort their interviewee because a more relaxed interviewee gives more quotable copy.

Doorstepping is only journalists trying to do their job.

Some might try to annoy and fluster you by:

- making provocative statements
- overstating the opposing view
- swinging between opposing viewpoints
- teasing and baiting with outrageous comments
- being cynical, sceptical and bold, controversial and argumentative
- asking probing questions
- trying to put words into your mouth, 'So, you'd say then ....'
- deliberately saying inaccurate things so that you will contest and argue
- rephrasing and re-asking a question until you answer it.

Expect all of this and you will not be surprised.

Some journalists:

- cultivate a reputation for being aggressive
- are looking for interviewees who are interesting, passionate about their subject and opinionated
- know that the best way to get a good comment is by being outrageous and polite.

Most journalists will be seeking to relax you and get you to open up, not to make you nervous so you clam up.

Successful interviewees:

- respond calmly
- ignore the absurd comments
- correct the ignorant or inaccurate statements
- can calmly ask where the journalist got their facts from
- get their messages into the answers, whatever the questions
- stick to their messages, but are able to follow the journalist's line of questioning
- use positive words and phrases
- avoid negative words and phrases
- do not repeat any misleading, statement in case that is misconstrued as agreement
- do not accept the interviewers misleading or false interpretation of events or facts, and can calmly put the correct point of view
- do not relax until the interview is truly over – which may not be when the journalist appears to be finished
- is not drawn into criticising competitors
- do not allow the journalist to put words into their mouth, instead of saying 'No, that's not what I said …'
- are not fazed by the journalist's silence … they either wait for the next question or start talking about messages, or new products, or something of interest to the readers
- will not be pressured into making a rash comment or quote by claims that the deadline is imminent
- do not fall for the surprise last question.

** Interviewees have to be prepared to let the conversation go the direction that the journalist wants … But at the same time, most journalists don't mind if the interview goes the way that the interviewee wants, especially if it leads to good copy. **

Good interviewees:

- look the part, using appropriate dress code
- sound the part, using professional and businesslike conversational techniques
- do not get flustered
- are well prepared
- have messages ready and written out
- will calmly make sure they know the journalist's deadline and publication, and phone number
- are brief
- are positive
- radiate an interested and interesting personality
- are lively
- display their knowledge
- don't use jargon
- are passionate
- are not afraid to say they don't know the answer
- are honest, but know they don't have to tell the whole truth
- don't need prompting about their views and opinions
- concentrate on the interviewer
- are pleasant and responsive
- remember that they are talking to their customers through the journalist
- use word-pictures
- will take control of the situation
- are not pushed into a defensive position
- try to achieve an equal balance of pushing and reaction
- do not to allow themselves to be flustered or bullied

- answer the journalist's questions and still get their message across

- feel confident enough to ask questions

- feel confident enough not always to answer all the journalist's questions if it is not in their best interests

- know they have the right to refuse to answer

- will attempt to answer the journalist's questions

- will flesh out their answer with messages and comments

- will use the journalist's questions to leverage their message into the story

- are not afraid to contradict, argue, correct or be firm in asserting their views.

** Keep your sense of humour and stay charming. Don't allow the journalist to provoke you. **

Good interviewees avoid questions they don't want to answer by:

- being charming, saying 'I'm very glad you asked me that, it's a very good question, but I think a more interesting question is ....'

- being frank, saying 'I'm sorry, I don't want to talk about that' or 'Sorry, I'm not the right person to talk to on that' or 'I'm sorry, I'm not empowered to talk about that. Perhaps you'd like to talk to my boss'

- refusing to answer the question as posed, saying 'Before I answer that question I'd like to say that ...'

- moving the interview on to something else, saying 'Well, that's an interesting question, but I think it is far more interesting to talk about ...'

- reinterpreting the question to suit their message, saying 'I think what you mean by that question is ...'

- refusing to accept the journalist's interpretation, saying 'You might say that, but my view is that ...'.

Watch out for inaccurate summaries of what you've said (i.e. 'so, you would say that …') If the journalist sums up inaccurately, put them right straight away. Allowing an innaccurate summary to stand gives it credibility and tacitly approves it.

Start an interview by making sure that the journalist:

- is properly prepared
- has their background facts right
- has your correct name and job title
- has your phone number and email address
- knows the name of the product and what it does.

Establish a rapport and don't bother with trivial greetings. Get straight to the point. Have your messages prepared, written out and rehearsed – keep them simple and avoid copious notes.

If a journalist calls unexpectedly …

You are sitting at your desk, working. The phone rings and it is a journalist you don't know.

Don't panic. You don't have to answer their questions immediately.

- Take control of the situation by finding out a few basics.
- 'Buy' yourself time to think and prepare.
- Thank the journalist for the call.
- Confirm that you do want to speak to them.
- Ask what they want to talk about.
- Use an interview check list to make sure you ask all the right questions, especially the journalist's deadline and phone number.
- Perhaps tell them that you are 'just about to go into a meeting – tell me what you want and give me your number and I'll call you back in five minutes'.

- Then call a PR manager or media-experienced colleague and ask:
  - what experience does this journalist have?
  - can you trust them?
  - how easy are they to talk to?
  - how knowledgeable is the journalist?
  - which publication do they work for?
- Write out the key messages you want to get over in this interview.
- Anticipate what the journalist might ask, particularly the difficult questions, and prepare and rehearse your responses.
- Call back when you have all the necessary information and messages to hand.
- Be prepared to email or fax over the latest press releases, case studies and facts.
- The journalist is unlikely to ask you exactly the right questions to elicit the responses that you want. Be prepared to steer the conversation down the route you want to take.
- Be prepared to 'brain dump' information as a seamless part of a conversation or interview.

** You are the expert – about your company, the product, its market and its potential. **

> ** When you are on the telephone to a journalist, they are likely to be making notes of everything you say. Slow your pace of delivery and repeat the most important points. Imagine the journalist at work. **

<< Listen to the journalist, determine 'where they are coming from' and deliver your message accordingly. >>

The journalist will probably have a preconceived 'view' or 'position'. It is usually a negative assumption, because that's the way most journalists work. If they start with a positive assumption and the interview proceeds with you both in agreement, the outcome will not be interesting to the reader.

During the interview, ask:

- what the interview is about (you might not be the right person to comment)
- which publication it is for (so you know who the target audience is and you can deliver the right level of technical or business content)
- the deadline (so you know how long you have to respond, and whether you can get back to the journalist later)
- who else the journalist has spoken to (so you have a better idea of the angle of the piece)
- whether it is news or a feature (so you know whether the journalist wants a snappy comment or a leisurely backgrounder or analysis)
- the angle the journalist plans to take (they may not tell you)
- where the journalist got the story (helps you determine whether the journalist is friendly).

Have your messages ready:

- Use brief prompts if necessary but don't allow yourself to become stilted or sound as if you are reading the messages from a script.
- Rehearse your material but don't learn it by heart – allow some room for spontaneity.
- Don't let your material come between you and the reader.
- Learn the facts, not the padding.
- Know your key points and practise saying them.
- Be as concise, succinct and clear as you can.
- Don't use three words when one or two will do.

- Don't be afraid of using emotional language.

- Illustrate your words with visual descriptions and anecdotes.

- Avoid flowery, waffly styles of speech.

- Avoid jargon.

- Use plain English.

- Be opinionated.

- Be a tub-thumper with strong views.

- Make it personal by using anecdotes, but keep them simple and short.

- Use metaphors and analogies to illustrate your points.

- Don't assume the reader has no knowledge, but do not patronise.

- If you feel passionately about a subject, let it show.

- Explain the thought processes which led to your views – don't just give conclusions. You are more likely to persuade the journalist if you explain everything clearly.

- Do not lie or deliberately mislead. But you needn't tell the whole truth.

- Round figures up or down to whole numbers – these are more dramatic and more memorable. Avoid fractions and decimals.

- Say the name of the company and product as often as possible – don't just refer to the product as 'it' or to the company as 'us' or 'we'.

Find out the journalist's view at the beginning by:

- asking what the profile of the reader is (from which you may be able to determine their angle)

- asking what the angle is (they may not tell you)

- asking what their view is.

** Don't ask the journalist to email or fax over a list of questions before the interview. This is standard practice in the US and really irritates UK journalists. They won't do it – and they'll go to your competitor to get comments or information. **

It sounds obvious, but *answer the journalist's questions.*

- The journalist will not know what you know – they are talking to you to find out more.
- Don't talk 'over' the journalist.
- Don't blindly push your message irrespective of the journalist's questions.
- Give the journalist an acceptable answer to their questions, then move the conversation on so that you can state your message.
- You are the expert – tell the journalist the most exciting things.
- If you persistently avoid the questions and push your own response, the journalist will probably think that you are trying to mislead them.
- The journalist wants you to listen carefully to what is asked and give an answer to that question.
- Don't just launch into a prepared answer which ignores what the journalist has said. A crucial part of being a good interviewee is to be a good listener. Absorb what the journalist is asking and think how you can skew the answer towards the message that you want to convey.

If you are too pushy the journalist may think you are:

- biased
- trying to spread propaganda
- trying to exaggerate the features or abilities of your product
- spreading misinformation which benefits you
- confused
- not as knowledgeable as you are pretending to be
- afraid to speak the truth
- deliberately hiding important facts or information.

End an interview:

■ when the journalist has all the information they need

■ by running through the main points of your message

■ by making sure the journalist knows how to get in touch with you again

■ by asking whether the journalist is working on anything else that you can help them with

■ by saying, 'Before you go, I'd just like to make sure that you know about ...' and then proceed to tell them something about your product or company

■ by saying, 'Before you go, is there anything else that you are working on that I can help you with.'

>>Return a journalist's call as soon as you have done a few moments' preparation. Who is the journalist, what is their publication, who is their audience, what are they likely to ask? Any of those you don't know, ask the journalist in the first few moments.>>

Have an efficient system within your organisation for dealing with enquiries from the press which includes the PR and marketing teams.

■ Use an interview check list to make sure that you get all the details you need from the journalist, such as name, job title, deadline and publication.

■ Make sure a report is circulated to all relevant managers, particularly to the PR and marketing staff.

■ Have a system for checking that the journalist receives everything they want after the interview and all follow-ups are actioned.

Commenting on the competition

The journalist may not be talking to you to find out more about you or your products – they may be more interested in your views on your competitors.

■ Avoid being too strongly opinionated or giving outspoken points of view on your competitors.

- The journalist will only be interested in negative comment.
- Be cautious.
- It is bad form to comment critically on your competitors.
- It is a cheap way to get press coverage.
- In the long term it does you no favours.
- Criticism of competitors usually comes home to haunt you.
- It does not make you look good.
- Unless your criticism is balanced and fair, it is better to talk about your product or company.
- Your tactic should be to positively promote your own position than to attack an opponent's.

To the questions 'What do you think about Company A's new product which they say is going to dominate the market in six months?' or 'What do you think about Company A's strategy to use cheap labour in the Far East?', you can respond with 'Well, I think it is a very interesting development, but more interesting is what we at Company B are doing with our new product' and then continue to talk about your product/company.

- In other words, side-step the question.
- Avoid being drawn, unless you have a balanced comment to make, such as 'Well, Far Eastern manufacturing does have some interesting benefits, but I think we at Company B would find that such a strategy would conflict with our policy on human rights.'
- You have made a comment on the question, but you have also introduced your message.
- The journalist may ignore your statement but at least you have avoided being drawn into a dirty war.
- If a journalist claims that a competitor is talking about you, ask for more details about what they are saying and deal with it point by point.
- You have no right to see the journalist's notes or to ask for transcripts, but courtesy and the journalist's Code of Practice might make the journalist oblige.

- Don't respond by making wild allegations about the competition.

- Think and talk positively about your position and assert your views over those of your competitors.

- Anticipate your competitors' views and opinions, and have responses ready.

- Have a short, positive statement which reinforces your message.

- It's not over until you are down the road – even when you are off-air, if you are talking to a journalist you can still be quoted.

Dealing with hostile questioning

On rare occasions you might find a journalist becomes aggressive or hostile. Usually such interview techniques are reserved for political interviews or for crisis situations, not for interviewees contributing to 'ordinary' news and features. The journalist is far more likely to be hoping that you will keep giving them lots of interesting and opinionated material. However, you should expect the journalist to criticise what you say. You cannot expect them to allow your statements or claims to stand unchallenged. That is their job.

The worst thing is to respond to rude or aggressive interviewing with aggression.

- Be calm.

- Concentrate on the positive aspects of your message.

- Don't restate an opposing view in your answer.

- Don't be defensive.

- If the interviewer tries to cut you off in mid-response but you really want to finish, try to do so. Say, 'Please let me finish', and then complete your sentence.

- Don't just say 'Yes' or 'No' – flesh out your answers, but don't ramble. When you are finished, stop.

- If the question is clearly far away from the subject and irrelevant but provocative, say, 'That's not what we are discussing here. What we are talking about is ...' or 'That's not relevant. What is important is ...'.

- Don't argue with the interviewer, or contradict them.

- Never lose your temper.

- Never walk out – it reflects more badly on you than the interviewer.

If the interviewer suddenly starts asking about a topic that you are not prepared for, say:

- 'That's not the topic I thought we were going to talk about and I'd like to get back to you on that one when I've had a chance to do a bit of research/I'm happy to talk to you about it.'

- Comment, but use phrases like, 'to the best of my knowledge' or 'as far as I can remember'.

If the interviewer says something inaccurate or unfair, don't let it pass. Both the interviewer and audience will respect you more if you assert yourself, correct mistakes and don't let false assumptions stand.

If the interviewer is very aggressive, the audience will have more sympathy with the interviewee. If the interviewee is arrogant, boorish, shows off or is dull, it is the interviewer who will come off best.

Radio and TV studio interviews

All of the above applies, but also:

- Arrive early to avoid being flustered.

- Do not take advantage of The Green Room hospitality (the Green Room is a 'holding' room for people going on and coming off. Frequently, alcohol is made available. Don't be tempted).

- Try to talk to the interviewer beforehand, although but it is most likely you will only be able to speak to the researcher or an assistant (the interviewer avoids talking to the interviewees in advance so that spontaneity is preserved).

- Ignore the microphone or other technical equipment, just look at the interviewer.

- Ignore lighting.

- Don't look at the camera.

- Dress for the occasion – it helps the interviewer treat you with respect, and makes you feel more authoritative, which comes across even on radio.

- Smile, even on radio, see above.

- Mention the name of your product or company as often as possible.

- Aim for sound bites – be succinct, repeat the question, stop when you are finished and don't ramble on.

- Speak in a normal voice – don't shout or 'drop' your voice to achieve gravitas like some politicians. The sound engineer will make sure that the sound level is okay.

- Practise a good delivery – clarity, good pitch, even pace, animation and emphasis.

- Be lively – don't try to hide your enthusiasm for the subject.

- Avoid 'ums' and 'ers' and unnecessary pauses.

- Open your mouth wide when you speak – don't mutter or mumble.

- Before you go on, limber up with a few facial exercises.

- Take a few deep breaths before you start.

- Avoid rushing your answers, but stop when you are finished.

- Warm up your vocal chords by imitating a didgeridoo.

- Imagine that you are speaking to an individual whom you love.

- Assume that the audience is wide and particularly avoid jargon or 'in jokes'.

- On television, don't refuse make-up.

- On television, lean forward slightly.

- On television, be careful not to look sideways or to the ceiling – keep your gaze constant.

- Keep hand movements to a minimum.

- Avoid touching your hair or face.

- A small amount of Vaseline on your teeth will keep your lips moving smoothly over your teeth – useful if your mouth dries through nerves.

- Keep looking at the interviewer.

- Don't worry about silences – it's the interviewer's job to fill them, not yours.

- It's all on the record.

- Don't just give 'Yes' or 'No' responses – try to rephrase at least part of the question in your answer, and give a good, rounded reply.

- Summarise your points at the end. If the interview is edited it is helpful and helps ensure that your main messages are selected for any trailer.

- Have respect for the interviewer but don't be sycophantic.

- Avoid familiarity with the interviewer.

- Use the interviewer's name.

- Avoid quoting numbers which overwhelm.

- Only use anecdotes and jokes if you are good at them. Don't suddenly launch into a story that you've just thought of.

- Don't be crude, rude or use swear words.

❋❋The interviewer will be wanting things to go well. That means they want smooth responses to their questions and short, well-informed answers. They wouldn't have asked you if they didn't think you'd be good. Just concentrate on the interviewer and try to relax.**❋❋**

Dress code for television:

- Button your jacket.

- Pull your jacket down sharply at the back and sit on the hem if possible. This prevents it becoming unattractively hunched around your shoulders and back of your neck.

- Good posture helps create a good impression.

Avoid:

- stripes

- loud colours

- small checks

- brown clothes

- bright white clothes

- Red clothing

- bare arms

- off-the-shoulder (for women!)

- bright jewellery

- badges, brooches or motifs.

> ** It's not the level of your voice that gives you authority, it's the content and what you say. **

Mobile broadcasts

Journalists are increasingly mobile, and an individual can easily make broadcast quality recordings or broadcast live with extremely small and portable equipment. Two people can do broadcast quality television recordings.

Mobile crews:

- can suddenly appear in front of you
- can suddenly turn up at your home or office.

You don't have to give an interview if you don't want to. If you feel unprepared, simply say, 'I'm sorry, I don't want to be interviewed right at the moment, I'll do it later.' Outright refusal or a brusque attitude will aggravate the journalist – the promise of an interview later is usually best.

Remote TV studios

Increasingly, TV stations use remote studios or broacast vans. The interviewee sits inside without the benefit of being able to see the studio or the interviewer. It can be a disconcerting experience, a bit like being in a photo booth.

- The technicians will tell you where to look.
- Imagine that you can see the interviewer or the audience, and smile as much as possible.
- Don't fiddle with the earpiece.
- Maintain the illusion of eye contact.
- When the light is on, you are on air.
- Play-act – give the impression that you can see the interviewer.
- You don't have to shout.
- The interviewer is not 'grilling' you, even though it might feel like it.
- Don't be defensive.

Phone-ins

The ultimate brief encounter – you have only seconds to get your point across so be very well prepared. If you can mention the brand of your company or product, you are doing well.

On and off the record

On the record is when a quote is attributed to a name. Off the record can be unattributed (the quote is used but no name is given) or given as background information (no quotes, no names).

The simple answer to the question, 'Can I trust the journalist not to use something I say is off the record?' is: 'No.'

But at the same time, journalists are generally trustworthy. They need contacts to get good stories, and their contacts come as a result of relationships built on trust.

Never say to a journalist you don't know well anything you don't want to see in the press.

There are times when it is useful to go off the record.

- When you want the journalist to know something but you don't want it attributed to you.
- Something about a competitor that you want the journalist to know but it would be bad form to have you attributed as the source.
- If you have a new version of your product in the pipeline, and you want the journalist to review it when it is available but you don't want it publicised yet:
  - because you have a stockroom full of the current version and it would ruin sales for the rest of the quarter
  - you don't want your competitors to know about the new product yet.

If you want to go off the record with a journalist you know:

- ask them before you say it, not after you have made the comment
- you need an agreement before the words are spoken.

Going off the record is an agreement between the two of you and it is a matter of trust.

- It is no good telling a journalist something and then saying, 'That was off the record, all right?'
- The journalist is not under any obligation to comply.
- Ask, and say, 'Can this be off the record?' and wait for them to say 'Yes' before continuing.
- The journalist may want to clarify the situation, and say, 'Does that mean that you don't want me to use it at all, or just not attribute it to you?'
- You may ask them to hold on to the information until a later date.
- Or the journalist may use the information but not name you as the source, or use the information as background facts but not refer to it directly.

Journalists know that off-the-record information can be useful.

- They can start working on a story before it becomes official.
- They can get a story quicker than their rivals.

Most journalists respect the relationship with trusted contacts and will not abuse their trust by printing something which has been given to them off the record.

However, you cannot assume a quid pro quo existing before you establish it with the journalist, and even then you have to trust them and cannot force them to comply. There are some journalists who put their career before all else and will do anything to get a scoop or better angle on a story. They will agree to something being off the record and then print it anyway.

- Do not attempt to go off the record in a studio or any place where there is recording equipment around.

- If the journalist agrees to go off the record, nothing you say should be written down or recorded

- It is a personal agreement between the two of you, and you have no legal right to sue if the journalist subsequently prints or broadcasts what you have said.

Most journalists will go to extraordinary lengths to protect a source who has put themselves on the line to pass on information, but some just treat off-the-record information as a chance to get a scoop.

Attribution

It is more effective for both the journalist and you if any comments can be attributed to a named person. Make sure that the journalist has:

- the name
- the job title
- the (full) company name
- the switchboard phone number
- the manager's direct line
- the company web address
- the manager's email address
- the PR contact name and number.

You should:

- check that the spokesperson's name and the product are spelled right
- the names are mentioned as frequently as possible throughout the piece.

Strictly speaking, journalists should attribute any remark which is not their own to the person who made it, and give the source of any quote which they have used, but they do not always do so.

Attribution gives a comment more weight and authority, especially if it is attributed to an expert.

Journalists are usually keen to attribute quotes. When the piece appears, you may find that the quote is attributed to you or your spokesperson with a verb like:

- 'so and so, marketing manager of SuperProducts Ltd, revealed'
- or 'Jane Smith, European export manager of Widget.com, asserted'
- or 'Peter Jones-Smith, managing director of The Best Products, claimed'
- or 'Mary Green, board director of Betta Widgets, attempted to explain'.

You have no control over this, despite the cynical ring they can give.

You may find that a journalist takes a press release or an emailed interview and puts other words in your mouth, attributing other comments that you didn't actually make but could have done, to you or your spokespeople.

Technically this is not good practice, but a great many journalists do it for the sake of time.

≪The PR can spend so much time agonising over quotes and getting the client to sign them off, and the journalist will chop them around. The truth is they often sound better when the journalist has edited them.≫

You should never ...

If you do or say the following you will look inexperienced and unprofessional.

- **Never thank the journalist for a piece which has appeared or been broadcast.** It makes the journalist think that it was not critical enough, that they missed something, or that they were too soft on you. They are not there to promote you or your product, but to satisfy their reader, listener or viewer – if you are pleased it means they didn't do a good job for their reader. You can, however, compliment them generally on the professionalism of the piece.

- **Never comment on the headline** – the journalist didn't write it, the sub did.

- **Never say 'No comment'** because it looks so bad. It implies that you have something to hide and is a tacit acceptance of what the journalist is saying. Better to adopt some avoidance tactics than say it. If you do say 'No comment' the journalist is unlikely to leave the matter alone. They can say, 'Why will you not comment?' and keep on until they get some reply.

- **Don't ask when the piece is going to appear**. The journalist probably doesn't know – they just have a deadline for delivery. The journalist, especially a freelance, is unlikely to know definitely when it will be broadcast or printed. And if they do know, things might be changed at the last minute. Publication is out of their control and not their responsibility.

- **Do not ask to see the copy before it is used**. You have to trust the journalist's professionalism to get it right. Asking to see copy or hear a tape indicates that you don't trust them. It also looks like you think you have the power to change anything, which is *not* the case. Once you've spoken to a journalist, you have no right to make changes.

- **Don't ask to be sent a cutting**. If you know which publication it is for, make sure that you read it or use a cuttings agency. Journalists are too busy to send cuttings or issues to people they quote.

- **Don't ask them whether they are going to use the story**. The journalist will not know for sure what the editor will do, whether the story will get used or even what the subs will do with it.

- **Don't ask for your photograph or sample to be returned**. Apart from the inconvenience and cost, which will alienate the journalist, you should charge such costs to your promotion and marketing budget.

- **Don't give any information which you do not want to see published or broadcast, or quoted back at you later**. The journalist is always working – assume everything is on the record.

- **Don't start rambling**. Stop when you have finished your statement and wait for the next question.

- **Don't waffle**. Keep your answers to the point, and long enough to keep the conversation going. Aim to answer the journalist's question and get across some point of your own, then stop.

- **Don't be evasive or repeatedly dodge the journalist's questions** in order to substitute the answer you want to see in print. The journalist may think you are trying to hide something, and it's irritating for the listeners.

- **Don't fob off the interviewer's questions and move on too quickly to your message** every time. It has a negative effect, and people will want you to shut up.

- **Don't lose your temper.**

> ** Journalists can be your best source of competitive information. They like to gossip, and are probably talking to your competitors. They can be a useful source of information, so don't be afraid to ask them what they know, or their views on the future. They'll probably be talking about you to your competitors some day! **

Chapter summary

- Prepare with interview check sheets and message summaries.

- Have your cue cards handy, with your snappy company and product messages.

- Mention your company name and product brand name as often as possible.

- Aim to take control of the interview situation. You are the expert on the subject, that's why you are there.

- Make sure you know the journalist's name, title they are writing for and deadline.

- Give answers as passionately and colourfully as you can – journalists love enthusiastic interviewees.

- If the interviewer says anything wrong, correct them immediately.

- Do not lie, exaggerate or mislead.

- Nothing is ever off the record (unless you know the journalist well, and even then ...).

- Radio and TV offer more opportunities for publicity because they can't re-use material in the way print journalists can

Case studies

Luke Black	Self-employed PR consultant, aged 40
Service	Works with a group of six PR professionals. Each has their own clients but they share resources and help each other out when necessary.
Clients	Luke moved to PR from journalism five years ago, and works with four FMCG clients he met when he was a journalist.
Target sector	Consumer and lifestyle press.
Objective	To raise awareness of all his clients and their products among prospective customers, both business and consumer, and industry analysts. Luke's problem is that his clients have extremely high expectations of him, particularly as he was once a journalist – they think he 'has the ear' of all his former colleagues and can tell them what to write.
Action	After several attempts to educate his clients, Luke resorted to a few days' media training for them. He sat in on each day and contributed to the sessions, developing his clients' messages with them and helping with the interview role-playing. The trainer emphasised the role that PRs play, and explained that Luke has no control over what journalists write.
Result	The clients realised that Luke has no power to influence the journalists and that he also needs them to suggest newsworthy ideas for him to promote to the media. They also realised that they have to be opinionated and succinct, and respond fast to requests for comments or information. As a result their relationship with the press, and Luke's effectiveness, improved.

Recommendations PRs with journalistic backgrounds often make better PR people as they understand the pressures and agenda of the media. They can work efficiently with clients on their messaging and interview techniques, and pitch their clients' story in a way most likely to appeal to the journos.

However, journalists always have to have their readers' needs and interests as their top priority, and this will invariably be more important than the wishes of the PR person. Any PR with a background in journalism should understand this.

Luke has to do more to manage his clients' expectations of him, and not promise anything that he cannot deliver. In particular, he has to emphasise that he has no control over what journalists' publish. He is more likely to gain his clients' respect by being honest and not building up false expectations.

Daniel Dale	Freelance journalist

Description Daniel is 31 and started his career with a sports management degree before a year's postgraduate journalism course. He worked for five years as a staff writer on a leading men's health and fitness magazine, then went freelance. He now writes for many national and specialist health and fitness magazines.

Task Daniel has to be pro-active in suggesting feature ideas to his commissioning editors. He has about a week's work ahead of him, but needs to get more work in. He decides to spend a day building up his commissions.

Experience Daniel starts by contacting those editors and feature editors he writes for regularly. He has a list of possible feature ideas, but has to be careful not to pitch the same idea to more than one editor. Although he aims for an economy of scale he has to watch his reputation among the editors.

Daniel also contacts a couple of editors he hasn't worked for before, and is rewarded with one short news commission and one long feature.

Recommendations   PRs need to be aware which commissioning editors like the journalists to pitch ideas, and which like to commission freelances to fulfil their ideas for features. In the latter case, the PRs have to concentrate on the commissioning editors as much as the journalists.

Computer-aided journalism (CAJ)

Introduction

The internet has created an enormous revolution in journalism. It has affected:

- the way publications are made
- the speed with which news reaches its audience
- the number, quality and type of publications
- the way that information is distributed to journalists
- the way that journalists research, interview and write their copy.

You need to:

- understand the new push/pull effect on the dissemination of information and news
- use the web and associated technology and services as PR tools.

** Don't try to insist that the journalist works the way you want to work. If they want press releases by email, fine, but not all do. Check their individual preferences and then for heaven's sake respect them. **

When using the internet to reach the media:

- Take into account the immediate and interactive nature of communications when planning to include it in your PR strategy.
- PR strategies must reflect the fact that companies and products will be under increased scrutiny because of the internet and it is harder than ever to control what is reported.
- Ensure that you consistently track the web for activity which is relevant to your company, market sector, competitors and products. The skill of online issue management is gauging which issues need managing.
- Remember it is a medium which can transform messages – once a message is out, the sender loses control.
- Be wary of engaging in narratives and conversations with journalists in chat rooms and conferences. Consumers and journalists often resent unsolicited intrusion by companies.
- Remember that almost anyone can set up a special interest group, user group or flame site. Monitor non-official activity carefully.

The internet is invaluable for:

- reaching journalists
- pitching ideas
- delivering information
- interviews.

You can use it for:

- virtual press rooms
- workshops

- debating forums
- technical support to journalists;
- web conferences
- online presentations
- systematic research.

However:

- not every journalist uses the internet
- not every journalist uses email
- some journalists prefer telephone or post
- email and the internet have disadvantages and limitations, despite obvious speed and cost advantages.

** The internet can certainly take the admin out of PR, but PR professionals risk becoming glorified call centre operators. The problem with electronic communication is that it cuts out the essential face-to-face relationship that PRs need to develop with journalists. Totally faceless electronic communications between journalists and PRs can isolate and dehumanise. **

<< Some PRs ignore those journalists who do not want electronic press releases or prefer emailed interviews, or even dislike using the internet at all. How silly. Think of all the opportunities they are missing, just because the PR doesn't like the journalist's favoured way of working. >>

** A surprising number of PRs try to shoe-horn journalists into their way of working. It alienates the journalists and ensures that the PRs miss a large number of key journalists. **

** Technology means that journalists can be part of the viral marketing process, spreading information electronically. **

Pushing information to journalists

The internet is fantastically useful for delivering information to journalists, but must be used carefully.

** You have to make life easy for the journalist, and encourage them to read your press release or click on the link to your site. **

You can use email to:

▨ deliver press releases

▨ circulate regular (weekly?) summaries of news and opinion

▨ respond to journalists' specific requests for information for ongoing news or features.

** Journalists get fed up with too much insolicited information, and infortunately the internet has just made it easier for PRs to load journalists with piles of rubbish. **

The internet has spawned a new category of media services which matchmake between journalists, publications and PR professionals.

There are:

▨ press release services

▨ features list services

▨ listings of journalists

▨ listings of freelances

▨ response mechanisms where journalists request information and comments from PR professionals

▨ expert opinions.

Examples are

www.sourcewire.com

www.prnewswire.co.uk

www.pims.co.uk

www.mediadisk.co.uk

www.profnet.co.uk

They offer either a:

- dissemination service for electronic press releases
- listing of freelances and staffers
- method for journalists to request information from PR professionals
- a combination of all these.

Using services like Response Source (*www.sourcewire.com*) requires particular skills and new protocols. You have to:

- tailor information to match individual journalist's requests for information
- respond fast. The technique is not as instant as the telephone, but it doesn't mean you can take days
- deliver opinions, views and facts which the journalists can use in their work
- not ask the journalist whether they want input from your client or spokesperson. If they have put a request on a noticeboard, assume that they want input from you. Just make sure you deliver it in the way they request
- not allow CAJ tools like Response Source replace more intimate and personal relationships with journalists. Keep building relationships with meals, etc. as well
- ensure that sufficient resources are allocated to managing and maintaining the site. It will have to be checked at least once a day, for example, and kept updated.

You also need to:

- have an electronic workflow system for reporting all contacts with journalists
- update the journalists' and publications' database daily
- have your spokespeople trained and prepared.

** The internet is invaluable to streamline, organise and accelerate everyday PR functions. If you want speed, responsiveness and agility when you are not driving your Porsche, use CAJ. **

Email interview

Eventually, voice-over-internet (VoIP) technology and broadband desktop videoconferencing links will enable journalists and spokespeople to conduct desk-based interviews using live video links. However, at the moment, CAJ interviews are limited to emails.

** More and more journalists are using email to conduct interviews. It means they can be more efficient in their work. They lose some spontaneity, but make up for that in other ways. Nothing will completely replace telephone and face-to-face meetings, but email offers an alternative which is being eagerly seized by both PRs and journalists. **

Email interviews are basically the same as telephone and face-to-face inteviews, and follow the same rules outlined in Chapter Six.

- The journalist will be seeking to entertain, educate and inform their audience.
- They will not be seeking to publicise your product for you.
- You have no control over what the journalist publishes.
- Don't just send press releases in response to specific questions.

- Keep your comments short, but when sending opinions, more is better than less, but not multiple, unsolicited attachments.

- Always ask a journalist before sending an attachment (some journalists ban all attachments – your database should say which).

- Be controversial.

- Don't agonise over getting your email word perfect – the journalist is bound to chop it around and take out what they want. Better to concentrate on being opinionated rather than being grammatically accurate.

- Include the name, job title, company name, switchboard phone number, company web address and personal email of the person to be attributed with the quotes.

- Use an interview check list (see Chapter Six) to ensure that you have the necessary information, such as name and contact details of the journalist, publication (so you know the audience) and the deadline.

- Send a photograph of the person to be quoted to the publication electronically and by snail-mail post with a note saying who it is and which story it is to go with. Don't send photographs to freelances, they don't need them.

Email interviews have other strengths and weaknesses.

Positive	Negative
Spokespeople have time to consider their responses	No control over what journalists will select to use
Fast, efficient and cheap	Backlash among editors who dislike copy written from emailed and boiler-plated comments – they see it as lazy journalism
Can include written words, with quotes,opinions, appraisals, reviews and recommendations, plus audio and video	A quick turnaround is essential – can be a problem for clients or senior managers who expect several days to compose their replies
Can include hot links to web sites and other email addresses	Some replies will have to be returned to the journalist within 30 minutes, others offer a week or more

Positive	Negative
Provides clearly defined briefs of what the journalist wants, and the deadline	You have no way of knowing whether the journalist found your responses appropriate or whether they will use some or all of your comments
Stock responses can be prepared in advance and stored. See Chapter Four, Message development part two to help develop your opinions on predictable topics	
	Journalists expect a 24x7 response
	Does not reach all journalists or publications
	Impersonal

** Just because you only see a couple of paragraphs in a feature doesn't mean that the journalist doesn't need far more than that to take extracts from. Send a few hundred words of strong opinion in response to each question and let the journalist pick the ones they want to use. **

≪ Some journalists really hate going to meetings and others really dislike the telephone. Email is heaven-sent for them. ≫

Electronic distribution of press releases

For many journalists and PRs, especially those in the IT sector, electronic distribution of press releases is now the norm. Many prefer them electronically because they can save them to disk, search on key words when researching, cut and paste information into stories and send releases to their colleagues.

However, others still prefer snail-mail post ones usually for logistical reasons (electronic press releases have to be downloaded and printed out to get a hard copy).

≪ The idea that journalists spend ages browsing through hundreds of electronic press releases is, frankly, absurd. Many journalists tell PRs they prefer electronic press releases because they are easier to delete – and the PRs have no idea. ≫

** Some journalists are receiving several thousand electronic press releases each week, and some PRs think that the journalist reads every one. At least, they tell their client that theirs is being read! **

<< Many journalists just delete all the electronic press releases they receive. And the PR has no way of knowing, but blithely tells the client that the journalists have received the press release. A great many PRs tell their clients that CAJ and electronic press release distribution is the way forward, and for some it is, but certainly not for everyone. >>

Positive	Negative
Cheap	No way of knowing whether the journalist reads them or keeps them
In theory, the journalist can store all press releases in one area on their hard disk and sort them according to key words when researching	Lacks the major advantage of snail mail which is that the brand or logo is passing over the journalist's desk on a regular basis
Lack individuality of snail-mail versions	Thoughtless emailing can be just as intrusive as thoughtless telephoning. Can be seen as spamming, which can be detrimental to brand and reputation
Record of how many hits to which press release, and how many picture files have been downloaded	

Electronic press releases should:

- be personalised
- have the title of the release in the subject line
- use upper and lower case, not all upper case – that is bad net etiquette and means you are shouting
- make sure the title and first paragraph are strong
- have links to relevant and recent online news stories that support your release

- be creative, but keep it simple with lots of bullet points
- have links to competitors' sites (a good journalist will know these anyway, but you get Brownie points for providing a useful service)
- have embedded meta tag information for filtering and archiving by news agencies.

Electronic press services

As well as services like FeaturesExec (*www.sourcewire.com*), which offers a list of up-coming features, there are electronic press release distribution services to targeted journalists, research report services and opinion summary services.

Electronic press release services will offer to write your release and deliver it to key journalists and publications in the sectors you want to target.

Electronic image agencies like PRshots (*www.prshots.com*), will create electronic libraries for you, distributing images in the right format to your target publications.

Positive	Negative
Apparently cheap (but can have hidden costs, such as indiscriminate or inaccurate list)	Whatever claims they make, are prone to flawed lists
Many services offer a post-distribution report showing which journalists clicked on the title of your release to download the full story	Can be expensive
	Some journalists don't like them
	Your release can be lost among many others

Press release distribution in-house

As an alternative to using an electronic press service, your department can keep a database of journalists' email addresses so that you can send out press releases yourself.

Positive	Negative
Cheaper than an agency	It takes time and effort to keep the list updated
Lists can be refined and releases tailored for each sector or each journalist	You lack the economy of scale of an agency or press release service

If you take the DIY approach, you must:

- make sure the address book is kept updated
- don't delete journalists who prefer snail mail
- avoid spamming (sending lots of unsolicited and unwanted emails).

Electronic press audits

There are two types of press audit:

- to update your journalists' database;
- to get feedback from journalists on your company, product or client. Asking journalists for their views can be helpful when developing a fresh marketing and PR strategy.

Positive	Negative
Cheap	No way of knowing why the journalist fails to respond
The journalist can respond at their leisure	No way of judging the effort put in by the journalist
	No way of validating seriousness or reliability of responses
	Unable to deviate from questions, as with telephone audits

These audits are traditionally undertaken by telephone or post, with mixed response rates. The internet and email offer an alternative method.

When running an email-based press audit:

■ never have more than five or six questions

■ give an incentive for the journalist to respond

■ avoid spamming.

E-invites

The internet can also be used to invite journalists to events, as an alternative to telephone or snail-mail invitations.

Positive	Negative
Cheap	No way of knowing why the journalist doesn't respond
Can be sent at the last minute if necessary	
Can be used as part of an invitation process and followed up with a telephone call to check attendance	Lack individuality of snail-mail versions
Efficient way to announce shows and exhibitions, and to encourage press registration	

The best e-invitations:

■ are for briefings rather than launches

■ are low on corporate hype and high on developing industry credibility

■ are used to build rapport

■ don't show the other journalists who have been sent the invite (make sure the invite list is 'blind copy').

The worst e-invitations:

- have memory-hungry logos which take a long time to download
- forget to include the date, location and instructions on how to get there
- omit to give the journalists a good reason for going
- don't list the speakers or who will be available for interview.

After the event:

- offer journalists the press pack electronically
- offer it to invited journalists who did not reply or attend.

Pulling journalists to you

Journalists increasingly use the internet for research and to find pundits for comments.

Your company web site

Journalists often check a company's web site as a first port of call when researching a specific company, product, general product area or market sector.

Positive	Negative
Offers a shop front for the press to learn about your company and its products	You don't know when the journalist has been there, or what they wanted, or whether they got what they wanted
Useful for crisis management – in the event of a story breaking quickly, or a damage limitation exercise to be implemented, a statement on the web site can help calm a situation	If unfriendly or incomplete, can have a negative effect
	You have no control over hostile or malicious web sites set up by competitors or malcontents. You have to continually monitor the web for trouble

** Journalists go to company sites and visit the press area with different expectations, for different reasons and wanting vastly different things. You have to aim to satisfy them all. **

** Do not surrender control of the site to the IT department simply because you are in a rush to get the media delivery online. **

Your site must:

- have a press area, known as your web press office
- be updated regularly (preferably daily)
- be user-friendly
- deliver all the information a journalist will need without having to telephone an agency or PR professional
- have hot links to the PR agency
- have hot email links to all key spokespeople
- have a relaxed and friendly style, not too formal.

The web press office should contain:

- all background company facts and statistics
- FAQs (frequently asked questions)
- the company mission statement
- everything that is in the public domain and the journalist could find out anyway through other means
- white papers
- graphics and statistics
- PDFs of company logos, brand logos and other images
- opinions on current issues – short comments with attributable name and job title

- opinion pieces for reuse

- web links to 'other recent articles by this author'

- summaries of the latest press releases with the option to see the entire release

- past press releases, with headlines and the option to view entire releases

- biographies of key spokespeople

- specifications of products

- company financial information

- email link to the product manager

- web links to reference sites and customers

- high-resolution (min 30dpi) photographs of relevant managers and products

- a thumbnail and the size of full picture file

- telephone numbers as well as email links.

Put as much as you can on the web site – just make sure the navigation flows easily and logically.

✳✳ If a journalist goes to your company web site and finds the press area, they want to be able to connect direct with the PR or marketing person responsible for press relations. ✳✳

Make sure that you reply to journalists' emails immediately, if not sooner. Follow up by telephone to make sure that the journalist got everything they wanted – it's a good excuse to call.

Your press area of your company web site should not:

- be full of turgid press releases – give a summary with hyperlinks to the full release

- be password protected – it just annoys journalists and deters those browsing.

You should also:

- consider giving trusted journalists access to your extranet or intranet
- have a compelling URL
- think about the media audience and what they want from your site
- have clear and measurable objectives (not easy with web-based media relations)
- ensure that your online brand reflects the off-line strategy and image
- aim to build a community of media professionals using your site. To do that you have to deliver value.

** Don't forget many journalists, including staffers, work from home and don't have powerful technology there. **

<< If a journalist asks a question, post the Q&A under the FAQs section on the site. >>

Virtual press conferences

These take the form of an internet-based interactive webcast, an event open to all, with written, live sound and live video links.

They have a poor reputation so far, but it is early days in this type of service and they are likely to become routine once supporting technology is available. They potentially offer great benefits.

The technology needs to improve before real-time online virtual press conferences using web-casting become a viable reality. The advantages to journalists and PRs are significant, so there is likely to be considerable investment in developing virtual press conference technology and acceptance. Specialist companies such as *www.simplywebcast.com* are helping make virtual press conferences and interviews a more user friendly medium.

Positive	Negative
No travel time or costs	Dependent on technology
Cost effective	Vulnerable to technology problems
Offer the ability to replay the conference over and over	Not all journalists have the receiving technology, especially freelances
Offer the ability to include customers and commentators from anywhere in the world	If more journalists log on than anticipated, the system can have problems
Allow multiple participation	Attempts at over-sophistication can backfire

It may not be long before PRs routinely use WAP (wireless application protocol) to deliver announcements, invitations and other information to journalists via their handheld devices or mobile phones. In particular, a filtered press release or news wire service could be delivered this way. The technology is already available, it is now a cultural and work practice issue.

** Maybe one day all journalists will log on to a few virtual press conferences every morning from the comfort of their desk, or even from their handheld device or mobile phone. There are big plusses and minuses. **

Journalists' web sites

Journalists' own sites give details of their careers and areas that they cover. Freelances can usually be contact via their web site. If you don't know their web address, experiment with their name, such as *www.anniegurton.com*.

** All journalists have email and most have their own web sites too. The web is the new shop window for freelances. **

> ** CAJ has several advantages, but PR is also about picking up the phone and talking to titles and freelances – coherently and in some depth, adopting at times the broad view – about ideas for editorial coverage, proposals for features and suggestions for pundits. **

Journalists also use the internet to communicate and chat with each other, and there are various forums for this. Some are closed and strictly for journalists only, but others will allow PR and marketing people in as well.

You could check:

- *www.1.cix.co.uk*
- *www.chinwag.com*
- *www.fleetstreet.org.uk*
- *www.net-media.co.uk*

There are also sites which are focused more towards marketing and PR professionals, some of which attract journalists as well, including:

- *www.audettemedia.com*
- *www.newmediamarketing.co.uk*

News web sites

The internet has spawned various web addresses offering edited news, unedited press releases or breaking news. These have varying degrees of credibility and usefulness. Their target audiences vary. Some are aimed at business managers and industry experts, some at researchers and decision influencers, others at the press corps.

Examples are:

www.theregister.com

reg@lettice.demon.co.uk

Pressmailing@butlergroup.com

www.butlergroup.com

www.multimediapr.co.uk/eunews.htm

Many sites have pro-active intelligent software agents and will alert the business manager or journalist when new stories arrive/stories arrive which include a predetermined element or key word.

Along with the lists of journalists, publications and programmes that you want to target, you will need to add the key journalists and news web sites. These invariably work to different deadlines and timeframes.

- Deadlines are more frequent.
- Stories can be updated almost continually.
- Journalists need even faster responses.

** Monitoring the media efficiently is almost an impossible task now, but it has to be done. The best approach is to imagine what news and information sites your customers are going to want to use, which news sites they are likely to be accessing, and make sure that those, at least, have details of your product and company. **

All the broadcasters and publishers have web sites, as do newspapers and many magazines. Often the editorial or summaries are available electronically. Electronic publications are always targeted towards the same audience as the main publication, such as the *Financial Times* and *www.ft.com*.

Editors and journalists on electronic publications and electronic versions of hard copy publications should be targeted, invited to events and kept informed just like any other editor and journalist.

- Web news and features are shorter than hard copy print stories.

- There is space available for more detail if required.

- Stories can give links to other sites and to email addresses.

- The sites can be searched on key words – for your own stories and your competitors'.

- Intelligent agent software can be set up to alert you if stories appear which contain key words.

- Innaccuracies in stories should be alerted immediately – they can be changed more easily in this medium.

- The journalists and editors often have web links to the stories for which they are responsible.

Internet-based press monitoring

The internet can also be used for cuttings services, and to monitor and track campaigns. There are various services available, such as

- *www.cyberalert.com*

- *ewatch.prnewswire.co.uk*

- *www.prism-online.com*

- *www.mediadisk.co.uk*

- *www.mediatrack.co.uk*

- *www.mediameasurement.com*

Online research

The internet offers a cheap and easy way to research the media, your audience and markets. However, there are cons as well as pros, to online quantitative research.

Positive	Negative
Inexpensive	Limited respondent 'universe'
Fast turnaround	Questionable issues surrounding sampling –
Automated data collection	narrow target audience, difficult to identify
Can show graphics and video	Potentially self selecting
No interviewer bias in data	Has to be on self-completion basis, which
High data quality with logic checks and open-	introduces doubt about credibility
ended questions	Prone to technical problems
Seamless international integration possible	

And for online qualitative research:

Positive	Negative
Faster and cheaper than traditional focus groups	Loss of verbal element of traditional focus groups
Avoids dominance by loud personalities	Less useful for emotive issues
More client control	Online moderation requires new skills
Can show concepts or web sites as part of process	Slow typing speeds or poor technical skills in respondents can create problems
Easier to recruit respondents	A narrow target audience can be hard to identify
Can be co-ordinated internationally or allow for surveys covering mixed nationalities	Sample can be hard to understand, and ensuring that group understands can be difficult to establish
	Prone to technical problems

Chapter summary

■ Most journalists use the internet.

■ You can use email and the web to deliver information, press releases, and find out what journalists are looking for and when.

■ You can use email and the web for interviews.

■ The internet offers a quick and cheap way to reach journalists, and for them to contact you.

■ You must respond fast.

■ You must have a press area on your company web site.

■ The press area must not have a password because it deters journalists.

■ The press area must be kept updated regularly and contain all the information that a journalist might want.

■ The internet has created many third party PR services, from features lists to response mechanisms, and cuttings, feedback and auditing services.

Case studies

Jane Jones	Senior PR account director, aged 38
Service	Jane worked in broad-based marketing for ten years before specialising in PR. She now works for a City-based agency that handles many financial corporates.
Clients	Jane's speciality is reputation management, taking care of the personal 'brands' of leading figures in the City.
Target sector	Business and financial media.
Objective	Several of Jane's clients are high-profile, big ego characters. One is a ladies' man, another is often in trouble with the police for substance abuse. Another keeps dubious company and another has a criminal record, which she is trying to put back in the cupboard. Jane is trying to raise the profile of each with the press, but in a positive way.
Action	Jane arranged a series of one-to-one meetings between key journalists and each client. Some were breakfast meetings, particularly for the more boisterous characters. She briefed them well and rehearsed them at length. She anticipated what the journalists might ask, and primed the clients so that each had two or three issues that they could talk to the journalists about. Nothing was out of bounds – the journalists were encouraged to ask whatever they wanted, and the clients were trained in how to deal with questions that could lead to negative press.
Result	The relationships between individual journalists and Jane's clients flourished, and the journalists started to initiate meetings and requests for comments. Because her clients are all

colourful characters they make good copy – provided they don't do anything too outrageous in the future.

Recommendations	Jane advises reputation management PRs to 'act fast and be honest, but you don't have to tell 'em everything'. Although encouraging close relationships between journalists and spokespeople that can lead to plenty of coverage, the PR has no control and it is a risky strategy.

Alice Tomorrow	**Sub-editor on a monthly yachting magazine**
Description	After getting a degree in English at Cambridge, Alice considered academic research but decided it would be too dull. Now her work in the leisure industry means she writes about people having fun.
	Alice is 27 and likes the backroom work of checking and rewriting copy, writing headlines and checking facts. Sometimes, when the editor is busy, she goes on press trips or covers press lunches.
Task	Alice has to write the copy for the contents page of the next issue of the magazine. She wrote the headlines and standfirsts last week. She also has to check all the phone numbers in the contact boxes at the end of the features.
Experience	Checking facts is one chore that Alice hates. She prefers to check them with the PRs because she finds that people are reluctant to give her the information she needs. They either try to sell her something or pass her on to another department. She even finds PRs can be suspicious of her motives. Eventually, she checks that all the phone numbers, emails and web addresses to be printed in the next issue are accurate.

Recommendations PRs and their spokespeople should know that when a sub-editor calls, they will not want an interview. They will just be checking a fact, such as the spelling of a name or a job title, or a phone number. Including all this information on the press releases could save much time, but even then the sub will still need to check. If a sub calls, be helpful and not defensive.

chapter

8

Following up

Introduction

Making contact, having an interview, sending a press release or just having lunch with a journalist is only part of the story. You then have to follow up. But you have to know how to follow up without being a pain in the neck and damaging the fragile relationship.

The problem is that if you have unsuccessfully pitched an idea, or once they have run a story, as far as they are concerned it is dead and gone – finished. So you have to be subtle and remember the rule: **Don't follow up without a very good reason – you must have something to add.**

≪ The relationship with the journalist is not going to flourish unless you work at it – you can be fairly sure that the journalist will not. ≫

You have to:

- build and maintain momentum in the relationship
- keep a regular flow of newsworthy stories coming through
- keep the angle controversial and opinionated
- aim to keep the journalist interested in your company and products with a continual stream of news, opinions and comments.

** Journalists have a well-developed air of prickly hostility which protects them from the most irritating, thick-skinned or determined approaches. **

Unless you have something interesting to say, which you genuinely think the journalist is going to be keen to hear, don't waste their time. Don't just ring up to pass the time of day or make pointless, time-wasting calls. Be aware that the journalist is getting plenty of other calls and has deadlines and other pressures.

** Don't bother a journalist unless you have a good reason to contact them. **

<< Most journalists prefer to deal with someone they already know, so once you have made initial contact, had a drink or met at an event, subsequent attempts at communication should be easier. >>

Journalists have antennae which alert them when a PR is lurking. Yet if you can hit it off with a journalist they can even be pleased to see you or hear from you. The trick is to treat them in a straightforward, businesslike way, and not be sycophantic.

Following up press releases

Clients or even experienced PRs might suggest that you 'just call up to see if the press release has arrived'. They are teasing you. Whatever you do – don't do it.

✳✳ Calling to follow up the press release is one of the initiation rites PR agencies inflict on novices, comparable to sending the new young lad in the builder's firm along to the ironmongers to ask for a bubble for the spirit level, or to ask for a long weight, or tartan paint, or a sky hook. Sometimes inexperienced PR people who don't know better will ring up journalists to ask whether the press release has arrived and whether it will be used (and can they be sent a cutting please?) and get a moderately polite response, but more often the reply is abrupt and to the point. **✳✳**

There are few things that irritate a journalist more than the question 'Did you get our press release?'. It's a joke in many editorial offices.

Remember that:

- journalists often get hundreds of press releases each week
- if everyone who sends a press release rang to check whether it had arrived, the journalist would deal with nothing else all day
- the press release has many functions, and 'being used' is probably the most superficial (see Appendix 3 on press releases).

Some PRs use other opening gambits, which journalists are generally familiar with and give the same short shrift, such as:

- 'We are having trouble with our post and we just wanted to make sure that the press release had arrived all right.'
- 'We forgot to include an important piece of information, and I just wanted to make sure that you have it if you need it' (such as the price).
- 'Do you need a photograph to go with the story?'
- 'Do you need a hard copy print-out of the research that the press release is based on?'

> ** If the story is a good one and the journalist has read the press release and is interested, they will follow it up whether or not you call them, and whether you like it or not. Calling them to see if the press release has arrived or to see whether it is useful is unlikely to encourage them to read it or use it . **

<< If the story is really good and strong, you can telephone the journalist when you send the release to warn them that it's coming. >>

This is something to be reserved for outstandingly newsworthy stories and not used for every release.

Following up press conferences

This is easier because it is more valid.

You can call to:

- check that they got everything they wanted for their story
- make sure they spoke to everyone they wanted to speak to
- see if they need any more photography or background material
- see if they have any queries
- see if they want to get together again
- meet the client, manager or spokesperson for breakfast or lunch
- see if they want to meet any clients or analysts
- see if they would like another interview
- see if they would like a complimentary sample of the product.

General follow-ups

Few journalists mind if you:

- make regular contact by email or telephone (whichever is the individual journalist's preference) to 'see if they are working on anything which you can help them with
- ask if they are looking for story ideas (they usually are)
- ask if they need people to quote for stories (they frequently will be)
- ask if they need any information on a story in the news
- offer users or knowledgeable experts for quoting
- offer analysts for comments and views.

Don't be:

- familiar, just because you've met the journalist once or twice
- sycophantic – sure to be irritating
- sales-ey – the journalist doesn't want to be sold to
- full of hyperbole and puff – the journalist will shut off.

Do be:

- business-like
- professional
- reliable.

** Many journalists welcome calls to offer comments on topical subjects and not enough people make them. **

You have to be prepared for journalists to be busy and rude, but even if you get a positive response from only one, it is worth making the call.

<< Even if the journalist is writing about your competitors, or especially if they are, they will be looking for comments. >>

But remember, it is bad form to criticise your competitors.

You should never thank a journalist for mentioning your company or product, it makes them feel uncomfortable and wonder whether they have been critical or analytical enough, but it is all right to call or email and compliment them on their brilliant copy or their excellent feature.

Become a source of information

Your aim should be to become the journalist's pundit of choice. You want them to call or email you every time they need a comment in your area of speciality. To achieve this you need to be:

- reliable – in the content of what you say to the journalist (if you tell them something wrong and they print it, it will reflect as badly on the journalist as on you)
- dependable – you are there when they call, available, ready to comment
- controversial
- able to talk about anything, off the cuff – go back to your messages, and look at the range of issues that you have opinions on. A good pundit or spokesperson will have comments ready on all the leading issues of the day
- quotable – deliver your views and opinions in short, snappy statements
- opinionated – deliver your views with passion, conviction and wit
- outspoken without too much regard for the consequences – people who are scared of getting into trouble will never make good spokespeople
- frank and honest – if you don't have anything to say, tell the journalist that. Hopefully, there will be another opportunity soon. The journalist is more likely to respect you if you are honest and say that you don't have a view on that issue than if you try to make it up as you go along
- willing to suggest new areas for comment – don't be limited to the issues suggested by the journalist.

** Aim to build yourself into a pundit or 'rent-a-quote' and this will effectively and quickly raise your profile and that of your product. **

Being quoted has a snowballing effect – the more you do, the more other journalists want you to do.

<< If you don't respond promptly in outspoken, quotable terms, you can bet that one of your competitors will. >>

Journalists go 'through' people – you might find yourself being quoted for a while and then dropped. This is simply because the journalist needs to continually find fresh people to quote. But this is also good for you – it means that others are always on the lookout for fresh faces too. You simply move from one journalist to the next.

Whenever you read something and think, 'I don't agree with that' or ' Why were we not quoted in that', don't just talk about it, *react*.

- Email/call the journalist who wrote the piece.
- Email/call the publication.
- Write a letter for publication.
- Ask whether there will be another similar feature soon that you *can* be included in.

If the publication has opinion pages, viewpoints or a letters page, the editor (or one of the staff – find out who) is probably on the lookout for new input or comment, so contact them and talk about it. But make sure that you have an idea of what you want to say first.

** The journalist is unlikely to call you and ask for your opinion – there are too many others being proactive about delivering comments on issues. You have to be proactive too. **

Competitions, offers

If the publication runs editorial competitions, special offers and sponsored pages:

■ first approach the editor. They will refer you to the right person to talk to. It might be a sales person and there might be a cost involved

■ there is frequently a liaison between the advertising and editorial teams regarding sponsorship

■ negotiate for good branding for your product, e.g.:
   – competition name to include your brand name
   – Flashes across the corner of the page
   – Flash on the contents page and front cover.

Some consumer magazines run a 'Letter of the week/month' award, with a tie-breaker and a donated prize in exchange for brand mention.

If the publication agrees to you providing a prize for a competition or best letter, etc., establish the ground rules. Many publications insist that you do not interfere with the judging process. Understand that your role is only to provide the prize.

✱✱ Some publications will give competition sponsors the names and addresses of all entrants, which provides a fresh mailing list of potential customers. **✱✱**

Other opportunities

Once a piece about you or your product or service has appeared, keep the story alive by stimulating and creating a debate about it or its sector, market, competitors or users. You could:

■ follow up with a letter to the editor or journalist, pointing out some element which was overlooked, or putting right any misunderstanding. By opening a debate you will keep public awareness of your product at a high level

■ offer editorial contributions such as opinion pages or case studies, assuming that you know the publication uses them. Don't get carried away with the sales puff and hyperbole, and commission a freelance journalist to write it for you – it is more likely to be in an acceptable style and format.

** Remember that the journalist is speaking to your competitors, customers and partners. They can probably tell you what your competitors are planning, and will tell your competitors what you are planning too. Gossip is the journalist's life blood – be careful with it but use it. **

If the journalist follows up

If the journalist contacts you after receiving the press release or after an interview or press conference, they are unlikely to be calling for a chat.

■ Establish the purpose of the journalist's email or call (they might be calling to check the spelling of a name, or a phone number).

■ Make sure you can satisfy their requirements before making promises.

■ Try to develop the conversation into other areas. 'Do you also know about our other products/Do you want to talk to our customers?'

■ Ask whether there is anything else that the journalist is working on that you can help them with.

Have an efficient system for dealing with enquiries from the press.

■ Use an interview check list to make sure you get all the details you need from the journalist, such as name, job title, deadline and publication.

■ Make sure a report is circulated to all relevant managers, and particularly to the PR and marketing staff.

- Have a system for checking that the journalist receives everything they want after the interview and that all follow-ups are actioned.

** Respond promptly to any contact from the journalist, even if it is to tell them that you've passed the request on to someone else. Later, check that others have responded promptly too. **

Chapter summary

- The press has to be told that you are available for comment.
- Don't follow up unless you have a story or an angle that will stand up.
- That story or angle has to be genuine and worthwhile.
- Don't ring up just to see if the press release has arrived.
- You can call to check that the journalist has everything they need.
- Follow up features lists.
- Make sure you are prepared with a strong opinion and some facts.
- If a journalist calls, you must respond as fast as you can, even if the deadline is not immediate. If not, you'll find your competitors have seized the opportunity.

Case studies

Sally Peters	Unemployed, aged 22
Description	Sally has just left university with a degree in Media Studies and wants to work in PR and marketing. Sally's areas of interest are sports and health, so she starts by contacting agencies which work in that sector. One agency offers to take her on for 'work experience' – they'll pay her nothing but give her the chance to work with PR professionals. If she proves herself, they might offer her a job.
Action	Sally feels she really needs the experience so she takes up the offer.
Experience	On the first morning Sally is given a list of journalists, their phone numbers and a telephone. She has to ring each one and ask whether the press release that the agency sent out last week arrived all right, and whether the journalist will be using it. If they say yes, she has to ask them to send the agency a cutting.
Result	After the first 20 calls she has hardly got past her introduction. Eventually a senior journalist took pity on her and suggested kindly that she shouldn't make any more calls. Sally decided that she couldn't take any more and didn't want to be a PR. Luckily, however, the agency staff decided that Sally had potential and took her off the job.
Recommendations	Sally should remember that first experience, and in the future, when she is in a position of more authority, she should intervene if a colleague sets up a work experience student to make similar calls. Not only is it cruel to the individual, it doesn't enhance the agency's reputation among the press.

Steven Pink	Staff journalist on the *Daily Chronicle*, an internet daily business news publication
Description	Steven is 25 and this is his third job, having started as a staffer on a local newspaper and then on a national Sunday. He is ambitious and wants to become an editor as soon as possible.
	The pressure on the mag staffers is intense. Steven comes in every morning to a clear desk and has to gather all the news from overnight news feeds, select the stories he wants to run, check them and do interviews, and write the stories. The site gets updated every 30 minutes, so Steven is continually sourcing, writing, checking, filing.
Task	The site earns revenue only from the banner adverts, and they will continue if the business audience continues to subscribe. Steven has to make sure that the site content appeals to them with a broad base of financial, business and corporate information.
Experience	Steven follows up on some company information fed to him by a PR contact. The story is fresh, big, and none of the nationals have it yet. On the basis of a telephone call and an email interview, Steven writes a story, which is picked up by the BBC. It runs the story in the evening news, and Steven's site is credited as the source. The result is publicity for the site as well as a coup for Steven – his subscribers were able to make adjustments to their financial portfolios before the stock market adjusted.
Recommendations	Journalists working on internet titles have special requirements, and appreciate being given news in advance. Although there is no legal support for an embargo, journalists working in fast-moving news environments are most likely to appreciate being given news with as much notice as possible.

chapter

Damage limitation

Introduction

With luck, you won't have to manage a full-scale PR crisis or implement a disaster management strategy. However, you may have to limit the damage caused by adverse publicity or a misquote, whether it is potentially a large-scale disaster or a minor blip.

Supposing:

- your product turns out to be dangerous
- there is an accident which is blamed on your product
- the journalist has misquoted or got their facts wrong
- there is a cock-up which results in bad publicity which threatens to damage the brand.

Because you have no control over what is printed or said in the media, you have to leave a lot to trust. Sometimes that trust is broken, either accidentally or intentionally. You need to know how to deal with the situation****

Damage limitation means keeping control of the impression given to consumers – it's all about rescuing the brand's reputation.

≪Anyone who is good at managing an enterprise should be good at reputation repair. The gap between operational management and reputation management is very little.**≫**

Part of a PR campaign is being prepared: you can't prevent disasters, but you should be prepared to mitigate the impact.****

How it can happen

Bad publicity can happen if:

- new products are rushed out without proper testing in an attempt to beat the competition
- wild promises are made which turn out to be misleading or inaccurate
- there is a mismatch between the company's marketing and sales and its actual product
- customer and user expectations are not properly managed
- spokespeople are not media trained and say the wrong thing to the press
- pre-announced deadlines or launch dates are missed
- the company or brand is linked with criminal activity, such as extortion, fraud or sabotage
- there are weaknesses in the operation which lead to public risk or threat to reputation.

A problem can be made worse by:

- disgruntled employees

- pressure groups

- activists

- alienated journalists

- unhappy customers who are more able to form into groups and exchange information using the internet.

<< Large orgnanisations can find that they have an 'attack' site full of grievances against them. There is little to be done about them. Best ignore them but try to address all the issues they are complaining about. >>

What to do

Act fast, act now and be truthful – but think before you tell the press the whole truth.

Speed and efficiency are key.

- Have PR radar which can spot a potential problem.

- Audit your crisis management strategy.

- Identify and define the problem before it becomes a crisis.

- Devise a strategy for dealing with it.

- Implement it.

- Anticipate the journalists' reaction.

- Have a strategy to deal with it.

- Implement it.

- Later, have a post mortem on why it happened.

■ Take steps to ensure it will not happen again.

✱✱Failure to respond quickly and efficiently to wrong assumptions or damaging impressions or statements can lead to an uncontrollable situation which then degenerates into an uncontrollable crisis.✱✱

≪Honesty is definitely the best policy – lie or mislead and you can make things ten times worse.≫

You may feel:

■ guilt

■ embarrassment

■ regret

■ despair.

But don't you let your feelings show.

Think about how you appear.

■ It is important to look good without appearing smug.

■ Don't look like you think you are untouchable – you are representing a firm or brand that is in the wrong.

■ Give an impression of confidence without complacency.

■ Accentuate the positive.

≪ A complaint to an editorial team needs to be handled carefully to avoid alienating the journalists with whom you will probably want to deal again in the future.≫

You should:

■ have a procedure in place that is ready to roll

■ keep your procedure updated

- do simulation exercises to test your procedures
- have a key spokesperson prepared, someone who can communicate key messages and stop misinformation
- spot a problem early on and nip it in the bud
- define your objectives and achievable targets
- decide on your complaints procedure and who you will contact
- make contact with the journalist you originally spoke to and communicate your problem
- assess the results
- escalate the complaint to a senior journalist or the editor only if absolutely necessary
- learn from the experience
- reassess your messages and rewrite if necessary
- take into account the status and needs of the entire business – you can't isolate PR from other departments
- make sure the web site is updated and reflects events.

Journalists increasingly use web sites as the first point of contact. Silence on the site either looks like incompetence or a denial.

≪ If there is a crisis going on, and you don't know all the facts or what messages the company wants to get across, don't talk to the press. Refer them to someone else. ≫

You must:

- admit the problem
- accept the reality
- make sure the right people do the right thing (e.g. the managing director being seen to take responsibility for a minor manager's mistake)

- realise the worst thing you can do is lie
- be straight
- apologise
- show remorse.

If handled correctly, an enterprise can emerge from a disaster stronger, with more integrity and better armed for the future.

Set up a long-term 'reputation risk management strategy' which includes:

- continual feedback on how the company, product and brand are perceived
- a response if feedback shows that reputation is being damaged.

The trick is to try and turn a negative situation around to your positive advantage.

What not to do

Try not to:

- ignore a problem or disaster in the making
- make promises or guarantees you can't keep
- be economic with the truth
- go to an interview with the intention of covering up. If you are invited to an interview and you feel that you are not going to be able to be honest, it is better to decline.

The key principles are:

- don't attempt to cover up
- don't tell lies

- don't avoid difficulties – deal with them

- say little, smile a lot and grab any photo opportunities

- offer to put the situation right as far as you can

- be sorry, apologetic and emotional without necessarily admitting liability. 'It's an awful thing that has happened, but it's really not our fault'

- reassure that you will do everything within your power to make sure that the situation does not happen again.

- make sure it doesn't happen again.

If the journalists have to resort to doorstepping, that's a sign that the corporate communications machine has broken down.

<< Doorstepping means that you have already lost the battle, and will have even further to come back to win the war. >>

Using the internet for crisis management

Every PR should have an internet management element to every crisis strategy for every client and product.

- Ensure your web crisis management strategy is reviewed and updated regularly.

- Remember that the internet is a 24x7 medium and that a crisis can arise at any time.

- If inaccurate, damaging or malicious comment appears in newsgroups or conferences, act swiftly to avoid the damage spreading to other parts of the web (the wider the untruths spread, the more likely they are to be accepted as fact).

- Take care when responding direct to newsgroups or conferences – avoid appearing as though you are trying to control free expression.

- Build at least one reserve site that can be brought online fast as part of a response to a crisis.

- Ensure that all internet activity is integrated into all other PR and marketing activity.

Complaining to journalists

Most journalists set out to produce a story which is accurate and fair. But it doesn't always turn out that way.

You may feel that your words have been distorted. **What appears is unlikely to be exactly what you said**. It is the journalist's job to sub and edit what people say to make their comments and quotes more readable. **It is probably far better, far more succinct and accurate**. You'll probably say to yourself, 'Did I say that?' with pleasant surprise. You probably used 'ums' and 'ers', jumped all over the place in your answer, and repeated yourself. A waffly, verbose quote is not going to make good copy.

This does not mean that the journalist can put words into your mouth, but they do have a degree of freedom to make your quotes appeal to the reader by being readable and arresting.

If you think that your product is unfairly criticised, the journalist is obliged to give you the right of reply. This is not a legal obligation, but any respectable journalist will give you the chance to write a letter for publication. The journalist is often also given the chance to respond to your letter of complaint, and you are unlikely to have the right of reply to that comment.

At worst, the journalist may take the opportunity to blast and abuse you or your product – they are in a position of power and if there is a personal vendetta then there may be some unfair and inaccurate reporting. Aim to keep good relations between you and the journalist – you may need to talk to them again.

- Speak to the journalist you first spoke to.

- Aim to get them to agree that they got it wrong.

- Ask for an opportunity to put the record straight.

- Only escalate the situation if the journalist will not admit that there was a mistake.

- Take the problem further up the line of responsibility slowly.

- The buck stops with the editor.

If you feel that you have been genuinely and unfairly treated, and your product sales have suffered as a direct result of a journalist's personal feelings, you can ultimately report the matter to the Press Complaints Commission.

You can sue for libel – and alienate the journalists.

✱✱ Do not think that the publisher can always overrule the editor. The editor has legal responsibility and the political relationship between them should mean that the editor has ultimate responsibility for editorial content. Going to the publisher over the editor is rarely fruitful and is likely to antagonise. **✱✱**

It is wise to do nothing for the first 24 hours after the piece appears. It is easy to make a kneejerk reaction to something which is actually only a minor error and does not really have any long-term ramifications. You need to be pragmatic – realise that drawing attention to a misprint or editorial inaccuracy can cause more publicity than letting sleeping dogs lie. Sometimes it is better to take the view that the damage is done and it is best to move on.

✱✱ It is not a good idea to threaten to stop your advertising or to actually pull your advertising. **✱✱**

It won't stop the journalist writing about you and may encourage them to continue to report negatively on your product. Your objective is to make a friend of the journalist, not an enemy.

Rights of reply

Journalists are obliged to give a right of reply to someone who has been criticised. Your rights extend to responding after the piece has appeared.

You can:

- write a letter for publication – keep it short and accurate, without laying blame

- negotiate a disclaimer or correction – you have to request that it goes on page 3 or even the front page, otherwise the box will appear near the back

- negotiate an agreed statement, as above

- discuss future editorial opportunities

- ask for damages, although these are unlikely to be given, at least without the threat of legal action. This can cause more negative publicity.

** You always have the right of silence. Although it can look bad and appear as an admission of guilt, in some situations it can pay to refuse to talk to the press immediately or issue a statement without further comment. **

<< A crisis can go global very quickly. You must have a crisis and reputation management strategy always ready. >>

Press Complaints Commission (PCC)

If you believe that you have been misquoted or facts have been portrayed inaccurately, and there is a refusal to correct or make a satisfactory attempt to set the record straight, or an alleged intrusion or bad taste, the Press Complaints Commission will investigate.

The PCC is a self-regulatory body set up in 1991 to deal with complaints against the press as one of the recommendations of the Committee of Privacy and Related Matters. One of its objectives is to make the press more culpable, although it has no legal powers above those already enshrined in the law.

Litigation

There are laws of libel, when someone's reputation is damaged by something which appears in writing or print. Libel is notoriously difficult to define, but the three best-known definitions are:

- a statement concerning a person which exposes them to hatred, ridicule or contempt, which causes them to be shunned or avoided or which has a tendency to injure them in their office, profession or trade

- a false statement about a person to their discredit

- a statement which lowers the plaintiff in the estimation of right-thinking peers.

The most common form of libel is when something is written which is actually true. Just because it is true does not mean that it is not libellous. The truth can be defamatory and can result in heavy damages.

> Personal stories told by a third party are a big danger. The journalist and editor are still liable to prosecution for libel, even if it is a reported quote. Not a lot of people know that.

Institutions and companies cannot be libelled. All libel cases are made against individuals. It is the editor of a magazine or the producer of a broadcast programme who will be deemed to be liable and will appear in court.

If you sue for libel:

- the editor might contest your claim

- the editor might maintain that the statements or quotes were true and accurate

- the editor might say that the story 'was told in good faith and without malice and in the public interest'.

Threats of libel are common – some journalists do not feel that they are doing a good job unless they attract the occasional libel threat. It means that they are upsetting people by printing things they do not want printed.

There are also laws of slander, when something defamatory is said or broadcast.

Chapter summary

- The PR professional has an important responsibility to ensure that a company's reputation is not at risk.
- If there is trouble on the horizon, get professional help.
- Don't lie.
- Admit to any problems, apologise, but don't necessarily admit liability.
- Express regret.
- Make reassurances that it will not happen again.
- If you are misquoted, consider whether it really matters before reacting.
- Write a letter for publication.
- Contact the journalist you spoke to, and be reasonable.
- Only go above the journalist's head to the editor if really necessary.
- Only go to the publisher if you really have to.
- Don't threaten to stop advertising – the journalists won't care.
- Put the incident behind you. Learn from it and move on.

Case studies

Jan Blank	PR assistant in the marketing department of an international conglomerate, aged 21
Objectives	Jan is one of five PR assistants. Her special responsibility is to maintain the database on publications and journalists, which means tracking the careers of staffers and freelances. She also has to keep features lists up to date.
Action	Jan has a busy and important job, if sometimes tedious. She has to develop relationships with as many journalists as possible, in a friendly and unsycophantic way – difficult when you are a junior PR in a large organisation.
Experience	Jan has found two ways to make her life easier – one is to work with other PRs, particularly external agencies which are keen to work with her company. As they have their own people keeping their journalists' database up to date, they feed the information to Jan. The other way is by using the internet.
Result	Jan is quietly efficient and works hard to keep the company's database up to date. They never send press releases to journalists who have left publications, and know exactly which journalist is responsible for writing which sections of the publications. This reduces their costs because there is no wastage and improves effectiveness because all press releases are well targeted. Jan helps write the releases too, and knows how to target each for individual journalists. It is time well spent and the company has a high reputation and good brand awareness.

Recommendations	Jan is a good example of a PR assistant whose attitude is leading professional and competent to relationships with individual journalists that will last her whole career. Jan should maintain her pragmatic and thorough approach to her job, even the boring aspects, and she will undoubtedly sow the seeds of success for her ambition to run her own agency one day.

Roger Barnes   Freelance features writer and columnist

Description	Roger is 65 and has started to cut back the amount of writing he does. He has a solid reputation with many commissioning editors and several regular commissions for columns and opinions.
	Roger specialises in board-level business issues. He is respected as a columnist and contributes to national newspapers as well as specialist business and management titles.
Task	Roger has to keep his columns fresh and readable, and knows he is competing with young staffers keen to fill his shoes. It is crucial that his comments, observations and opinions are relevant to the readers and as topical as possible.
Experience	As an old hand, Roger has plenty of long-standing contacts and he spends more time keeping in touch with them than he spends writing. Using email, telephone and meetings, he spends most of his working time networking and 'keeping an ear to the ground'. The result is that his columns stay readable and in demand. Feedback suggests that many readers turn to his columns first and so he is always in demand by commissioning editors.
Recommendations	PRs have to court characters like Roger. He is cynical, critical, knowledgeable and charming, good company and a devastating writer. But those who are able to interest him in fresh stories with a good angle for readers will find that their clients are amazed by the

coverage that they are able to get. He never gives overt product or company mentions, but even criticism from Roger is deemed to be good publicity.

10

The role of PR professionals

Introduction

By now you should have the confidence and ability to get editorial mentions. All you need is some experience. But if you still feel unsure, or do not have the time to devote to the task, an in-house or external PR professional will do nothing else but work with journalists on your behalf.

Theirs is a strange role: their clients pay them but they are the servants of the press.

✱✱ PRs are paid by their clients or employers but have to regard the journalists as their number one priority. **✱✱**

PR professionals generally have a bad press:

- their loyalties are often divided and confused
- the PR industry traditionally attracts a certain dishonest, sycophantic, empty-headed type
- many PR professionals irritate journalists because they continually push their client with little sympathy for the journalists' agenda.

> ** Journalists recognise that there is nothing as valuable to them as a good PR professional They are a resource to be used. **

Journalists' view of PR professionals

The relationship between journalists and PRs is often fraught and full of antagonism. Many journalists:

- dislike PRs intensely
- resent the fact that they need PR professionals
- think PR people are crass, guilty of misrepresentation and generally irritating.

However, a good relationship between a PR person and journalists is extremely valuable and productive, and:

- can help journalists get better stories
- can help journalists get better quotes.

Good PRs know the two cardinal rules.

- Do not waste journalists' time.
- Do not tell them lies.

The best PRs try to build good working relationships with journalists, entertaining them and only calling when they have something genuinely interesting. They know that the relationship is symbiotic and two-way.

** PRs cannot help resorting to hype or soft-selling – they think it is their responsibility to enhance information to try to 'sell' it to the press, without realising that this alienates them from the journalists and inhibits the development of good, long-lasting, mutually satisfying relationships. **

Bad PRs:

- are often guilty of hype
- attempt to sell to the journalists
- are guilty of heavy-duty pressure
- attempt to spread propaganda
- create resistance and antipathy among journalists
- are too familiar
- think it is part of their job to make overblown exaggerations about the company, product or people they are representing. Such grandiose claims can be counter-productive. Journalists have sensitive antennae which alert them when they are being told exaggerated or untrue things about a product, and they switch off.

PRs have to respect the professional distance between them and the media. A PR's client is the person who pays them; the journalists' client is the audience they write for.

- Just because you have one meeting or conversation with a journalist, do not think that you are best buddies.
- Journalists are meeting lots of people all the time.
- Never telephone and introduce yourself with just a first name, use a surname too.
- Journalists are not lifelong friends if you have only met once or twice.
- It is important for you, the journalists, your clients and the journalists' readers to keep a professional distance between you.

In-house versus agency

There are pros and cons to using an agency, doing your media relations yourself or using someone employed in-house.

	Positive	Negative
In-house	The PR department will be privvy to confidential information which an outside agency can never be told More cost effective	They cannot be fired as easily as an agency Will lack the loyalty of an in-house person
Agency	Can offer a greater pool of skills	The client is competing with others clients for executives' time The client never knows exactly who will be handling their account – the account will be won by principals and then passed back to junior executives to run and manage Often more expensive than in-house Costs are easier to break down and quantify – fewer hidden costs

It's a partnership – between whom?

While it is the client company which pays the salary of an in-house PR professional or the agency fees, the PR's true clients are the journalists they deal with.

- There must be trust between all parties.
- Journalists are unlikely to trust PRs.
- Clients have to listen to what PRs tell them (e.g. the news does not warrant a press conference, or you do not have a strong enough news story for a press release).

It is up to the PR professional to tell the client what the journalist really wants and to protect the journalist against the enthusiasms of a näive client.

<<The most important relationship to the professional PR person is the one between them and the press. They would rather lose the client than risk that relationship.>>

No professional PR person wants to jeopardise the relationship between them and the media.

One of the benefits of agencies over in-house is that agencies can be fired. Some clients believe that it is healthy to keep changing agencies every year or so. Others think that you should only change agencies – or at least get others in to pitch for your account – if the incumbent is becoming stale or not giving you the attention you expect. After a while agencies become complacent or have newer clients to which they give more time.

On the other hand, by sticking with an agency you will develop the strong bonds and long-term understanding necessary to work together effectively on a press campaign.

When the agency first pitches for the business, the potential client should insist on meeting the staff who will be handling their account and make it clear that if there are staff changes they reserve the right to move to another agency.

- Successful partnerships with PR agencies depend on personal relationships between the client and the account handlers.
- The client must have a clear and realistic idea of what is achievable.
- The agency must be recruited and appointed at an early stage of the product launch, not as a last-minute afterthought.

A good PR strategy involves more than just getting as many mentions in the press as possible. An agency should offer:

- business objectives
- milestones
- penalties for non-achievement
- measurable evaluations
- regular reports.

They should not:

- make promises to you or the press that they cannot keep
- wheel you out in front of journalists without good reason and preparation.

** Ultimately, the press is not your audience – it is the conduit to them. ******

What PR agencies offer

Despite being told they are shallow, superficial and cosmetic, good PR professionals perform an essential function in the relations between the press and members of the public. Many editors and journalists rely on good PRs for the smooth running of their publications.

Some PRs think they have a function to:

- cover up
- distract attention
- neutralise criticism.

They also provide invaluable help in:

- oiling the wheels of the publicity machine
- bringing products and people to journalists' attention
- achieving media mentions.

They can also be blamed when things go wrong!

PR professionals will help select the key titles and journalists that you need to approach.

The agency's primary objective is to help you win the hearts and minds of the journalists so that they think of you and your product favourably.

The agency will:

- plan your media campaign for you
- implement it with continual feedback and reports
- monitor the results
- make sure that you are trained appropriately
- help you develop the messages that you want to convey to the press to build a positive image and reputation
- anticipate any difficult or obvious questions that the journalists might ask. Even better, they will help you rehearse your replies to difficult questions
- co-ordinate a campaign so it matches advertising and other promotional activity.

PRs can select the right journalists for one-to-one meetings or lunches, brief the media to make sure they know in advance what your product does and who you are, and brief the journalists on any controversial issues to ensure that they ask the right questions so that they can get a story out of the interview.

They will sit in on interviews to help you get your messages across and make sure the journalist has a clear, accurate understanding of your product. PRs act as a buffer between you and the media. They will guide you on the right strategy, so you must listen to their advice.

The PR professional will spend their time monitoring and tracking journalists, publications and feature and news opportunities. They work closely with journalists and should have a good working relationship with your key journalists.

Measuring PR effectiveness is a thorny topic.

■ Some people doubt whether it can be done in a tangible way.

■ Others believe that it can be done and it is essential to do so.

The client needs to decide whether column inches or good relationships with journalists are their priority.

> **PR is a lousy form of marketing for lead generation, or for converting leads to sales. Do not even try to justify it on those grounds. What PR is good for is providing collateral material for the sales force and corporate image building, especially necessary for new companies and products. Do not even think that PR leads to sales, though.**

Selecting the right agency

You could:

■ ask a friend or colleague who has used an agency for their recommendations

■ contact the Public Relations Consultants Association (020 7233 6026), which has a computerised referral scheme called Preview that helps match people and their products with the right agency

■ ask working journalists which agencies they like to deal with.

Short-list those agencies which:

■ have a high percentage of ex-journalists on their staff

■ are highly regarded by the journalists you want to target.

Asking the agencies to pitch

Arrange for two or three agencies to pitch to you so they can demonstrate what they can do and persuade you to hire them. This is a two-stage process.

■ Brief them with what you want.

■ Inform them how much you want to pay.

- Tell them your expectations and experiences.

- Be frank about any problems.

When they do the pitch presentation, you can expect them to tell you:

- what they will do

- on what timescale

- for how much.

If you ask more than four or five agencies to pitch, you cannot expect them all to give you their full attention. In fact, it can be counter-productive to ask too many to pitch. Just ask two or three, and make it clear to them that it is a competitive situation.

- Look for an agency which indicates that it intends to learn your business.

- Look for one which promises continuity of account handlers.

- Make your choice based on the individual account handlers, not the overall agency.

- Pick one with a track record for getting good publicity.

- Talk to their past and present clients.

- Agencies which have former journalists on the staff are almost always the best.

- Many agencies charge to pitch, which is professional, realistic and avoids time-wasting. If the agency is going to invest the necessary amount of time in the briefing, preparation and presentation, and make the process worthwhile, it is fair to expect to pay them. At worst, some people take the agency's ideas without using the agency. Usually, the pitch fee is deducted from the first bill.

You want an agency that:

- respects your budget, and does not spend money foolishly or carelessly (e.g. executives who always get taxis when tubes are quicker and cheaper will spend your money faster)

■ takes the creative process seriously (and doesn't just go down to the pub to help stimulate the creative juices, or insists on expense-account lunches)

■ has stable staff (who are not going to leave next week so you have to brief someone new)

■ does not just use junior staff as dogsbodies or in place of senior staff (they need proper training, and are not substitutes for experience)

■ does not have more clients than it can manage

■ does not have clients much bigger than you to whom they will give preference

■ needs your business

■ is respected by the journalists (ask them).

Getting the most out of your PR agency

Buying PR services is a commercial activity like any other and it's up to the buyer to beware.

To achieve a happy marriage between you, the client, and your PR agency:

■ be clear about your motives for hiring the agency in the first place

■ be clear that what you are buying is their time, expertise and access to resources which you would not otherwise have.

Once you have appointed an agency:

■ spend time fully briefing the executives

■ agree measurable objectives

■ listen to their advice

■ agree a timescale

■ agree points of contact

- have regular reviews, at least quarterly

- make sure the agency is well co-ordinated internally

- if it is agreed that changes are necessary, make sure they happen

- respect your agency's views and expertise.

The biggest single reason for a breakdown of relationship between agency and client is false and unrealistic expectations. Sometimes agencies create false expectations in their pitch.

False expectations can be avoided by careful briefings, discussions and the setting of agreed objectives.

To work with an agency long term, you need to:

- motivate the PR team

- give feedback

- recognise good work

- monitor the workload and expectations

- measure performance according to mutually agreed milestones

- recognise the ultimate impotence of PR people to control journalists

- continually monitor and evaluate the agency's performance.

You can only measure the effectiveness of a media campaign when you have an appraisal, strategy and plan to start from, against which measurement can be made. Regular reviews and appraisals are essential for an effective long-term relationship.

Review questions can include:

- Does the agency reach the right audience?

- Are you improving your performance against your competitors as a result of the PR?

- Are your competitors also being properly tracked?
- Have your strengths and weaknesses changed since using the agency (i.e. fewer weaknesses)?
- Does the PR investment deliver value for money?

> ** Monitoring and measuring the agency's performance is only the first stage. Then you need to act upon your observations and effect improvements and changes as necessary. **

Measuring PR effectiveness

There are two types of measurement:

- How effective your PR strategy and activity is in terms of editorial coverage.
- Whether your PR generates sales.

It is extremely difficult to measure the effectiveness of your PR agency, but you need some kind of yardstick.

** If you can't measure it, you can't manage it **

Without some kind of measure you can easily begin to feel dissatisfied with the PR performance.

Ten per cent of every PR budget should be spent on:

- research
- pre-planning
- evaluation of the campaign.

Best practice guidelines suggest that better planning and evaluation are crucial to successful media relations and product promotion. Campaigns should be planned and measured against business objectives as well as media impact. Increasingly directors are moving from measuring the cost of PR to the impact of their expenditure – there has to be a definable business benefit.

PR budgets are soaring, but too many agencies have a wasteful, scattergun approach.

Techniques to measure PR effectiveness are:

- focus groups
- opinion polls
- customer surveys
- media analysis
- media audits
- customer feedback.

PR has traditionally resisted index-linked work, but this may be because so many campaigns have little or no impact.

But part of the payment should be linked to the achievement of specific business results.

There has to be some way of monitoring whether the company's messages – about its business performance, its brands and products – are reaching those audiences it specifically needs to hit.

PR is ultimately uncontrollable because the journalists are uncontrollable.

<< Press activity can be extremely random and it is hard to make it accountable and numeric. >>

There are three basic options.

- *Column inches,* a crude but reassuring and visible yardstick.
- *Weighted measurement,* in which column inches are measured against the cost of getting the coverage, taking into account various factors such as how many people read the publication and whether they are the target audience.
- *All-in,* in which some measurement of intangibles and long-term press benefits to a favourable view and mention of the product are taken into account.

** There is a direct correlation between the number of times a message is exposed to a target audience and its effectiveness. **

Other agencies use complex algorithms to produce statistics on the 'frequency' and 'reach' of a message.

Whichever you choose, it has to be agreed with the agency or in-house PR profes-sional. You have to have a methodology which is fair and fits all your objectives.

** Any agency that is spraying its client's messages around indiscriminately will miss its target audience. **

There are tangible benefits, including column inches, and number of times the brand or spokesperson name is mentioned. But there are also 'soft benefits' or 'intangibles' which are crucial to raising brand awareness – and are extremely hard to measure and evaluate.

** PR professionals are adept at shovelling thick folders of press cuttings in front of their clients and directors. They might look good, but they don't mean much. **

Media mentions can be coded for evaluation purposes, according to:

- the size and impact of the headline
- the overall size of the story and the power of the hook

- the prominence of the story in the paper, programme or schedule
- the strength of the content and the editorial focus, compared with stories surrounding it.

You have to determine in advance the value of every mention according to how much a comparable advertisement would cost. This needs to be set against the cost of obtaining the mention, using this formula:

- the total value of the mentions in terms of the cost of comparable advertising against
- the total value of sales generated by the publicity activity.

This figure needs to be set against and compared with the outcome of this formula:

- the total value of sales generated by the publicity activity against
- the total cost of the activity.

However, this approach, known as 'return on investment', does not take into account the intangible benefits of effective press relations. Some believe that the only way to continuously track the market's perception of you, and how much of that is down to your media activity, is to undertake continuous market research. However, this is expensive and usually impractical.

Most PR agencies offer a media evaluation service, which is usually based on quantitative and qualitative elements.

Quantitative evaluation counts:

- the number of mentions
- the column inches
- the number of publications and programmes.

Qualitative evaluation measures:

- the tone of the comment
- the degree of understanding of the press and reader or listener

- the context of the mention and whether it was mentioned alone or with competing products. For example, some mentions are trivial and primitive, while others may be brief but extremely valuable because of their timing or placing.

A simple 'How did you hear about us?' question to new prospects can help identify potential customers attracted to the company by its PR.

The ultimate measuring stick is whether the PR produces new clients and increases sales.

That might be unfair on the PR professional who didn't design the product, set the price, make the sales pitch, or write the contract, but a fair measure is still how many leads are generated.

You should also conduct similar audits and track your competitors' media efforts. Know how much time and money they are spending on working with journalists, and how much editorial exposure and product sales they are getting as a result. Also note the tone of their editorial.

Software programs and web services are available to track and report on the media coverage, correlating that with sales leads and actual sales, and to compare with competitors' activities.

Chapter summary

- Journalists don't love PR people, but they know they have to live with them.
- The best PRs are often ex-journalists.
- However, few journalists would be seen dead taking on a PR role (or 'taking the PR shilling').
- The worst PR people are sycophantic, creepy, over-familiar and incompetent.

■ The best PR people are business-like, know not to waste a journalist's time, and know what the journalist needs.

■ The best PR people value their relationship with the media more highly than their relationship with the client.

■ When selecting a PR person, check with a journalist whether the candidate is well regarded by your target journalists.

■ Agency people are easier to fire.

■ You have to tell your PR what you want, and push them until they deliver.

■ Listen to your PR – they know the media better than you do.

■ Agree your expectations at the outset, and monitor the relationship regularly.

Case studies

Ellen Taylor	PR in a high-tech PR company, aged 31
Service	Uses technology to respond to IT-savvy journalists.
Task	To provide responses on behalf of clients to journalist enquiries which come via an internet PR response mechanism.
Experience	Ellen sent ten email replies to journalists requesting input. Three contained unsolicited images of the product, which almost caused a freelance journalist's system to crash in downloading them. Several emails suggested clients to interview to journalists seeking product stories. As Ellen began to run out of time, some of her emails to journalists had no introduction and simply contained an attachment. These journalists had enough responses from other emails and did not risk getting a computer virus by opening these attachments. One email gave a succinct introduction to a product and how it would fit in with the feature, offering images and interviewees on request; the journalist emailed back requesting further information later that day.
Recommendations	Ellen needs to take an intelligent look at the positioning of clients' products for each feature. Ellen should not have bombarded journalists with email attachments, but noted what was available, e.g. images, further press releases, and acted quickly when these were requested.

Roshni Patel	Freelance features writer, aged 36
Description	Roshni is a home office-based freelance journalist writing for specialist business and consultancy publications. She does a lot of her background research from the internet and because she is based in a rural area and has family responsibilities she rarely carries out face-to-face briefings

Task	Roshni has to write a 3,000-word feature on the state of the ebusiness market for a highly respected publication. Her deadline from the magazine is in ten days but she wants to finish the piece in three days because of her family commitments.
Experience	She requests leads and interviews from a number of PRs. She prefers telephone interviews or email requests for interview. She asks for contact by email because she does a large proportion of her work outside office hours, but despite this two PRs telephone offering face-to-face briefings.
	One PR sets up a relevant interviewee that same day. However, at the end of the 30-minute telephone briefing the interviewee asks when he will be able to see the copy to check its accuracy. The editorial policy of Roshni's commissioning editor is not to allow copy approval, so the time spent doing the interview has been wasted.
Recommendations	PRs need to pay close attention to the way a journalist wants to work if they are to get their clients featured. If email contact is requested, don't telephone. Clients should be trained to understand that approval is not generally an option for editorial copy.

1

appendix 1

Myths and facts

Press releases don't work and are a waste of time.

It's true that journalists get hundreds each week (sometimes hundreds every day) but they are still an essential way to get your message across and are an important part of every media campaign. They have to be written in the right way, though – a press release aims to inform, not entertain.

Journalists get their stories by following their hunches. Pushing your product story doesn't lead to editorial.

Journalists get stories from all kinds of sources. Many have their origins in contact from PRs.

Journalists need me more than I need them – they like to deal with PR people.

Wrong. You can't get editorial publicity without journalists writing about you, so arguably, relationships with journalists are the key. Journalists have to deal with some inept and persistent PRs, and to many journalists PR people are a necessary evil.

I should ring up and ask whether the press release has arrived/whether it is going to be used/when it is going to be used.

Telephone the journalist to ask whether the press release has arrived – and be prepared to be curtly brushed off. *Never* ring the journalist to ask whether the press release has arrived or whether the journalist will use it.

I should check with every journalist whether they want to receive my latest press releases.

No, just send it to journalists working in your target market area.

If I put 'Embargo' at the top of the press release, the journalist will think it is something special.

No, the journalist will evaluate it in the same way as they look at all press releases – in about ten seconds. And they will not necessarily respect an embargo if they really want to use the story.

I should send a photograph with every press release.

Only if you want to waste your budget. Send photographs only to those who might use them, such as staffers. Freelances are unlikely to use photographs. They can always ask for them if they want one. Some magazines choose their stories according to which has the best picture, so make sure the publications get photographs.

I don't understand the technology, but I'm sure the journalist will.

No. If you can't understand it, don't send it. Don't assume the journalist has highly technical knowledge – chances are they don't, even if they are working on a technical publication.

I can make my press release eight pages long. That will make fascinating reading.

No. Only the headline and first paragraph are crucial, the rest is for quotes and brief background information. Limit your press releases to a two-page maximum. If the journalist is interested they will call you for more information.

If I send my press release by fax it will catch the journalist's eye.

Only if that is the way the journalist has requested to receive press releases. Otherwise, faxed press releases cost the journalist money to receive and are a nuisance.

I should send my press release by fax, email and post to all journalists – a scattergun approach is bound to have some success.

No, better to be well targeted. Your database of journalists should tell you how each journalist prefers to receive press releases.

In these days of high technology, I can send my press release by email.

Only if that is the way the journalist has requested to receive press releases. Some like to receive them by email – they are easier to delete without reading. Some like to archive them without reading them, and sometimes will search on keys words if they are researching a topic. Some dislike email press releases because they don't read their emails regularly and they have the inconvenience of downloading them. Email press releases are cheap and easy for PRs to distribute, but send snail-mail ones to the journalists who prefer them that way.

I have a great idea. I'll send the journalist three or four teaser press releases before the real one, so that they know it's coming.

No, you will only irritate the journalist. If you've got a story, tell them. Don't try to tease.

I must follow up every day.

No, but you should keep in regular contact with journalists you know. Don't keep pushing a story which the journalist is obviously not interested in.

If I ask the journalist when a piece is going to appear and which page it will be on, I can place my advertisement next to it.

No. First, the journalist is unlikely to know exactly when and where the piece will appear, and second they will not want to tell you even if they do know. Professional journalists like to keep advertising and editorial apart.

If you mention to the journalist how much you are spending on advertising, it encourages them to give more space to your product review and the quality of the report.

Not if the editorial is respected. If the publication does offer you editorial linked to advertising spend, you should question whether the editorial will have any value with the readers. Journalists often react negatively to any suggestion that they might write differently if there is a worthwhile advertising budget.

If you send a bunch of flowers or bottle of champagne with the press release, the journalist will use the story.

Not necessarily. They will probably welcome the gift, but if the journalist is any good it won't make any difference to whether the story is used or to the degree of prominence it is given.

If I tell the journalist something confidential which might get me in a lot of trouble, they will protect me and not reveal me as the source of their information.

You can't rely on it. Protecting a source should be a fundamental principle of journalism but unfortunately some judges have decided that it may be in the public interest that a journalist's protection of their source is less important than the right of companies to discipline staff for speaking out to the press, or for sources to be made public. A journalist may be forced to reveal their source, even if they don't want to.

If I tell the journalist about my fascinating new product, they will be enthralled.

Unlikely, but possible. It is more likely that you will have to spell out the benefits and implications so the journalist can clearly see the story and its relevance to their readers.

If I don't put the date or job title of the spokesperson on the press release the journalist will have to call up to check – the journalist is looking for an excuse to talk to me anyway.

No, it will go straight into the bin.

If I don't give the journalist some of the sales information, they won't understand what my product can do.

Give the journalist the information, but cut out the sales talk. You are not selling to the journalist and they can tell when you use hyperbole and 'PR puff'. Keep it business-like and straight – many journalists find marketing speak highly offensive.

But my product *is* the best/largest/cheapest/first.

Only make those claims if you can back them up with independent research and analysis. If you have such data and statistics, use them.

If I send my press release to as many journalists as I can find, surely I stand a better chance of some of them using it.

It will be a waste of your PR budget to send everything, including photographs and sample products. to everyone. If you want a campaign which gives good return on investment, target your mailing and make sure that you only send photos and sample products to those who might use them.

I don't need to read every single magazine. If I just contact the journalist they can judge whether the story is suitable.

When you speak to a journalist you must be intimately familiar with their publication and know every section, the who writes which section, the type of story they use and their deadlines.

While I'm talking to the journalist I can ask whether there is anything else they are working on that I can help them with.

Yes. Chances are, there is. This is a good closing question to an interview or meeting.

The magazine has just come out and, despite taking the journalist out for lunch and promising a free sample of the latest product when it's lauched, we aren't mentioned. I think I'll complain, and perhaps even stop my advertising.

Taking the journalist out to lunch and offering a gift will not ensure that your story is used, and anyway, it's not up to the journalist what is used. The journalist will submit their copy to the editor who passes it to the sub-editor and either may have removed that section or the piece. Perhaps the journalist did not use your quotes – they may not have been interesting or relevant to the reader, in the journalist's view.

By all means call the journalist and ask why, but only to learn from the experience, not to complain. And pulling your advertising? No, it will not change the situation and you will aggravate the journalist. Media sales and editorial are kept apart on all respectable publications.

Freelances keep changing job. They are not as important as staff writers.
No. Freelances are more important. They write for more titles, they are more experienced and they are more likely to be career professionals. A relationship with a freelance should be viewed as a long-term one. Make sure they are well briefed and kept updated on your product.

Journalists are mainly stuck at their word processors. They don't get out much. They don't meet many people.
Some don't. But you can be sure they are talking to your competitors and probably have a wide grasp of the market. If you have a story to tell, take the journalist out for lunch and talk to them about your competitors.

Freelances have plenty of time to come to lunch and go on long trips.
No. For freelances, time is money. While they probably appreciate hospitality as much as or more than staffers, they have to justify time spent away from their desk.

Freelances don't need White Papers or case studies.
They may not use them verbatim, but the chances are they will find them useful for background information. If you have any such material, send it to the freelance.

All journalists work in different ways.
Yes. Different in the way they approach their work, their attitude to deadlines, subject matter, preferred angles, audiences and specialisations. Your database should detail each one's preferences, including how they prefer to receive

information. Note all kinds of snippets about their family, hobbies, likes and dislikes. Update the database after every contact.

Journalists only ring up a few people for quotes. They have their favourite contacts, and there's not much chance of them contacting me.

Naturally journalists have their preferred contacts who they know they can rely on to say something quotable, but you should be aiming to join that group. Be outspoken, opinionated, able to take a broad overview, and able to back up any claims with facts.

I'm organising a press trip. I'll put the journalists in economy class while I travel with the client in first class. It means that journalists won't be forced to compromise their integrity.

And will ensure that the journalist has a low impression of you and your client.

I was so pleased with the piece the journalist wrote that I think I'll telephone and thank them for mentioning my client.

No. If you do that, the journalist will start wondering whether their piece was critical enough. The journalist is not there to please you but to satisfy their readers, viewers or listeners. Thanking them is unprofessional. You could compliment them on the piece in a general way ('That was an excellent piece of journalism ...') but do not thank them directly for any publicity they have given you.

I love gossiping with journalists. They really know everything that is happening.

Yes, most journalists like to gossip, but remember that they might quote you, however informal the situation might be.

Surely the journalist is off duty some time?

As far as you are concerned, no. Always regard a journalist as working, unless they are truly personal friends.

A journalist needs me as much as I need them.

Yes. They rely on people like you for comments on topical issues, information, and ideas for stories.

I sent the journalist a sample of the product. They haven't reviewed it or mentioned it so I think I will ask for it back.

Asking for demos and products back is tacky. Best to write off the cost. You gave it to them – leave it with them. If they were thinking of mentioning your company or product, they won't after you've asked for it back.

The journalist hasn't mentioned the product I sent them. Should I call and ask them why?

No. You could perhaps call to make sure it's working properly and they have all they need, but don't hassle them about when any mention might appear. Be pragmatic – your asking won't make any difference.

Editors want to be wined and dined.

Probably, but only if you are good company and don't expect anything in return. Otherwise, it is a waste of time. Remember that editors are not necessarily the ones who will be writing the copy. It may be better to spend your hospitality budget on the journalists who are badly paid and will be the ones actually doing the writing. If you don't expect anything in return for your hospitality, you might get it.

I'll send a review copy of my product by courier to the freelances with instructions to deliver before 7am – they'll be grateful for the wake-up call.

No comment.

My company has a new version of my product and we are very proud of it. If I hold a press conference, the media will be keen to be there and sure to report on it.

Unless you are a global company with a product announcement of world-shattering proportions, your press conference is unlikely to attract many journalists, if any. Even those who do turn up are unlikely to write about it unless it has implications for their readers, viewers and listeners. Don't bother. Think of another less stressful, more effective way of getting the news of your product upgrade to the media, and make sure you have a strong angle or hook.

To get a journalist's attention I have to be outrageous.

You have to have a good story and some interesting views and opinions. Create a lot of noise or use novelty marketing techniques and you are more likely to irritate.

Publicity is a matter of luck.

A bit, but experience and timing are more important. There are so many things that you have to get right and so many ways that you can get it wrong, that luck does come into it. You have no control over what the journalist will report, no control over what else might happen to affect the story, so luck is an important element. But experience and timing are crucial too.

I'll offer to check the journalist's copy for mistakes.

Only rarely will the journalist let you see their copy before publication, and then it is only likely to be to check for accuracy if the piece is highly technical. Demands to see copy are sure to be refused.

The press is out to get everyone.

Some may be on a witch-hunt and behave like rottweilers, and some enjoy the power and the pen in giving bad publicity to those who have irritated them. But the good ones are just looking for good stories for their audience, and that means they need to be critical and independent. They won't necessarily give you an easy time, but their reason is not just to be vindictive.

It will be Christmas soon. I think I'll send every journalist on my database a plastic pen, a corporate calendar and a mouse mat.

Those who send generous gifts will do so without any expectation of editorial or even that the journalist will remember them – but they will hope that human nature and courtesy will prevail.

For more hints and tips on how to handle journalists' FAQ, visit *www.honk.co.uk/fleetstreet*

2

PR and journalists' contacts and services

ABC for measuring hits to your web-site *www.abce.org.uk*

Advance Features. Forward features list 0870 736 0012 *www.mediainfo.co.uk* or *www.advancefeatures.com*

Audette Media. Electronic PR discussion site *www.audettemedia.com*

Benn's media directory. Lists all newspapers and magazines in the UK 01732 362666.

Brad. Media contacts for journalists. 020 7505 8273

Broadcast Monitoring. News alert service 020 7247 1166 *www.bmcnews.com*.

Broadcast Monitoring. National and international live monitoring 020 7963 7600 *www.tnsofres.com*

Central Press Features. Content for newspapers, magazines and web sites 0117 934 3604 *www.central-press.co.uk*

Chartered Institute of Marketing. Provides knowledge and career information to marketing and PR professionals 01628 427 500 *www.cim.co.uk*

Durrants. Cuttings service and broadcast monitoring 020 7674 0200 *www. durrants.co.uk*

Echo Communications Research. Measuring PR strategies and results 01483 413 600 *www.echoresearch.com*

Editorial forward planning. Entertainment, daily and current news, and a press planner service 020 7440 8550 *info@forwardplanning.co.uk*

Evaluation Toolkit. Service from Mori that evaluates press coverage 020 7689 9494 *www.testresearch.com.uk*

FeaturesExec. Electronic features lists 020 7720 1222 *www.featuresexec.com.*

Freelance journalists' listing. Service from sourcewire.com 020 7720 1222 *www.featuresexec.com*

Foresight. Future events information, including product launches, conferences and exhibitions 020 7440 8550 *www.profilegroup.co.uk*

Future Events News Service. National diary news service covering UK, city and world events 020 8672 3191 *www.fens.com*

Google.com. Research and site location for journalists *www.google.com*

Hollis. Press and PR annual listing of news controls and information sources for journalists 020 8977 7711.

Impacon. Media analysis 020 8579 0911.

Institute of Public Relations. 020 7253 5151 *www.ipr.org.uk*

Journalists' Directory at FeaturesExec. Where freelances find work, PRs find freelances able to do PR writing, where journalists look at press releases and where journalists contact PRs when they are looking for input to features 020 7720 1222 *www.sourcewire.com*

Liquid Media. Source of quotes, notes and news for journalists *www.mediamap.com*

Mantra. Planning and research services 01206 396665 *www.mantra-int.com*

Media Information. Provides various services to PRs 01494 797 252 *www.mediainfo.co.uk.*

Media Manager. Online contacts management system from PRNewswire 020 7490 8111 *www.prnewswire.co.uk*

Media Monitoring. UK coverage from Parker Bishop 01903 534 400.

Media Research. Broadcast monitoring service 020 7731 2020 *www.media-group.com*

MediaTrack. Evaluation and reporting on strategies and campaigns 020 7430 0699 *www.mediatrack.co.uk*

Media Training. Journalists visit PRs and their clients for one-day course 01727 875 325 *media.training@anniegurton.com* or *www.anniegurtonmediatraining.com*

Media Training. Public courses in central London 020 7490 7280 *www.pma-group.co.uk*

Media Week Directory. An online directory of consumers and B2B magazines *www.mediaweek.co.uk*

Metrica. Analysis for improved PR effectiveness 020 7922 1670 *www.metrica.net*

Moreover.com. An aggregator of news stories *www.moreover.com*

National Union of Journalists. Journalists' trade union 020 7278 7916.

NewsDesk. Internet-based news distribution service 020 7490 8111
www.prnewswire.co.uk

Online News. News service and resource for debating online journalism and
CAJ *www.journalists.org*

Pims UK Media Directory. List of newspapers and magazines 020 7226 1000.

Press Gazette. Trade newspaper for journalists *www.pressgazette.co.uk*
020 8565 4478.

ProfNet Global. Collaboration of information offices to give journalists access
to expert sources *www.profnet.com*

PRNewswire. Press release distribution 020 7490 8111 *www.prnewswire.co.uk*

PR Planner. Names of editors and journalists, with up-and-coming features
020 8882 0155 *www.mediainfo.co.uk*

Press Watch. Media monitoring and evaluation 020 7928 7688 *www.press-watch.com*

PR Organisers. Data and contact management 020 7354 7059
www.prorganiser.co.uk

Press Quotes. Over 400 spokespeople and journalists registered
www.pressquotes.com

PRshots. Stores images and photography for PR departments and distributes
them to the media in the correct format *www.prshots.com*

PR Week. Magazine for PR professionals 020 8267 4429 *prweek@haynet.com*

Public Relations Consultants Association (PRCA). Professional association.
020 7223 6026.

Release distribution and event monitoring at SourceWire. Events diary accessed by journalists, press releases sent direct to journalists' desks 020 7720 1222 *www.sourcewire.com*

Romeike. Analysis and consulting PR and media strategies 0800 289 543 *wwww.romeike.com*

Simply Webcast. Webcast service for press conferences and meetings 020 7430 4500 *www.simplywebcast.com*

Sirius Media Services. 01449 736 889 *grnfarm@globalnet.co.uk*

SourceWire. Service for PRs and journalists to make contact for information, views, opinions and contact 020 7720 1222 *www.sourcewire.com*

Taylor Nelson Broadcast Monitoring. National and international live broadcast monitoring 020 7963 7600 *www.tnsofres.com*

Two-Ten Communications. Media directories and listings of publications and journalists 020 7490 8111.

UKPress. A resource for journalists and PRs to discuss areas of interest *www.ukpress.org*

WebPR Newsletter. Aimed at PR professionals focused on CAJ *www.mediamap.com*

Willings Press Guide. List of magazines and newspapers 01494 797 300 *www.mediainfo.co.uk*

Writers' & Artists' Yearbook. A&C Black, London 020 7758 0200.

Books and sites on writing and journalism

The Elements of Style, William Strunk and E.B. White Allyn & Bacon, USA, 1979.

Waterhouse on Newspaper Style, Keith Waterhouse: Viking, London, 1989.

English Our English (and How to Sing it), Keith Waterhouse: Viking, London, 1991.

Winning PR in a Wired World by Middleberg *www.aurettemedia.com* or *www.amazon.com*

The Media in Cyberspace (www.middleberg.com)

Useful reference

Fowlers Modern English Usage, edited by R.W. Burchfield: Oxford University Press. ISBN 0–19–869126–2.

Roget's Thesaurus, Longman or Penguin. New edition prepared by Betty Kirkpatrick MA. ISBN 0–582–89363–1.

The Writer's Handbook, Macmillan, published annually.

UK Marketing Source Book. Directory with marketing and business information sources and including UK government organisations, Chambers of Commerce, libraries, online database hosts and consumer organisations. NCT Publications, PO Box 69, Henley on Thames, Oxon RG9 1GB, 01491 411000.

Writers' & Artists' Yearbook, A&C Black, London. ISBN 0–7136–4721–3.

Writing and delivering press releases

The importance of effective press releases can never be underestimated.

Press releases are:

- a primary method of informing the media about your company and product
- crucial in alerting journalists that you have spokespeople with relevant views and opinions
- an alert message to the journalist, calling 'Over here, I've got something to say'
- the backbone of your media campaign
- part of a co-ordinated media campaign, along with presentations, meetings, product reviews, etc. (see Chapter Three)
- a way to get your company name and brand across journalists' desks on a regular basis.

> ** **Press releases are as important now as they have ever been.** **

Press releases can:

- achieve better media coverage
- prolong coverage and raise levels of awareness
- result in immediate editorial coverage
- contribute to long term awareness building
- help educate the media and their audience
- go straight into the bin
- be saved for reference
- be included in an ongoing news story or feature
- result in a quote from the release being included in a story
- result in an email or call from a journalist for more information, a photograph or an interview
- establish credibility
- be informational
- limit damage in case of potential PR disasters.

However, be aware that journalists get a great many press releases – some publications get several thousand each week. Nevertheless, they are still crucial.

** Many PRs seem to think that journalists actually read each press release all the way through. How naïve. It would be physically impossible. **

<< Many journalists delete all electronic press releases without even glancing at them, and PRs have no way of knowing. >>

The successful press release is one which arrives at the right place at the right time with the right story. The trick is to ensure that they are written well and delivered accurately.

** The key to successful press releases is unknown, but the key to failure is trying to please everybody. **

Writing a successful press release is a critical PR skill, yet many either have no idea how to do it right, or bow to the wishes of the client to cram as much background information into the first paragraph as possible.

A surprisingly high number of press releases are mind-numbingly dull. How the PRs think that they will grab the journalists' attention and stand out from the sea of other releases is hard to imagine.

Press releases have to:

▨ grab the journalists' attention in the headline, standfirst and first paragraph

▨ quote an arresting opinion, fact or statistic in the headline.

Positive	Negative
Low cost publicity creation	No guarantee of coverage as a result
Serve many short and long-term functions	Extremely competitive
Ensure the brand name and logo get in front of target journalists on a regular basis	Are usually subbed – rarely used in entirety
Can be retained by journalist and used as part of wider feature	Quotes and information can be taken out of context
Editorial has more weight than advertising – perceived as independent	No control over how, when or where content is used
	No feedback over whether used, whether appropriate, or why not used

Constructing the press release

First and foremost: press releases must inform, not seek to entertain.

Press releases are like news stories. They should:

- come straight to the point
- be short and succinct
- deliver the most interesting part of the story first
- follow with more information
- include quotes
- end with background facts
- have all contact email addresses and phone numbers of all principals, as well as PR contacts, quoted in the release.

The first paragraph is the most crucial.

** Journalists only scan the headline and first paragraph and if you haven't caught their attention, then they will bin your release. **

The first few sentences have to answer the questions 'Who' 'What' 'Where' 'When' 'Why' and 'How'.

- Who is the story about?
- What is the story about?
- Where is your product available, or where is the event being held?
- When is it happening?
- Why is it interesting, or why is it happening?
- How does it work?
- And most important of all: *What is the benefit to the customer or user?*

Do not overload the first paragraph by trying to answer all those questions at once. Select the most important, which is probably *the benefit to the user or customer.*

** When the journalist reads a press release, the first thought in their mind is often: 'So what?' You have to make the relevance immediately apparent. **

The journalist will ask:

- Why is this story going to interest our readers?
- What has happened?
- Where did it/will it happen?
- When did it/will it occur?
- Who is involved: which company or individual?

You have to:

- concentrate on the facts in descending order of importance
- present the story in a clear, digestible form
- put only one idea in each sentence
- express yourself positively without jargon or hype
- ensure the press release is part of a wider campaign
- be prepared with your response in case a journalist follows up and makes contact.

Press releases must have:

- a clear hook (usually the benefits to the potential customer, or relevant statistic or quote)
- controversy
- appropriate timing (not to arrive too late for inclusion)
- relevance (to the journalist's audience)

- topicality
- a newsworthy element, and

to overcome the 'So what?' factor.

Press releases have to be targeted.

- One press release will be inappropriate for all journalists in all markets.
- You have to define:
  - the type of journalist, e.g. staff or freelance, news or features, market specialist or generalist
  - the type of publication, e.g. trade or consumer, weekly, internet or monthly
  - the analyst or customer who will be reading the release or the resulting story
- You have to tailor several versions of a single press release to suit several types of journalist and audience.
- The press release must contain newsworthy information, and not just be a sales letter dressed up.

Practical rules

Although PR professionals have personal preferences, most journalists agree that a release should:

- be one-and-a-half spaced (single spacing is too tight and double spacing uses too much room)
- be two pages long (one is too short and three or more is too much)
- be on one side of the paper only (not printed on back)
- have contact name and phone number only (not all contact details) on the front page in case the pages get separated.

In addition:

- use the company logo
- head the first page 'press release'
- do not use 'for immediate release' (what else would it be for?)
- give it a headline
- a standfirst
- use bullet points as much as possible to make text easy to read and accessible
- use colour to highlight
- put background information on second (and last) page – can be single-spaced
- all contact information should go at the end, including email and phone details for all spokespeople and principals as well as PRs
- offers of photography, sample products, further information should go at end
- pages should be stapled together at the top-left corner
- put date of release at the start and end
- include web addresses for further information at end, with appropriate URLs for research on story
- for real appeal to journalists, give competitors' URLs too.

✱✱ There is no need to write the company history and mission into the press release. Swamping the journalist with too much information is counter-productive. Keep it simple. ✱✱

- You can use letterhead notepaper. Spending money on special paper printed with the words 'Press Release' is not essential – it is the story that counts.
- Use spot colour or photographs to catch the eye.
- Use colour in the printing, but plain white paper – coloured paper is distracting, not eyecatching.

The hook

Press releases can be used to announce:

- financial results
- a new company division or merger
- change of name
- new product
- new appointment/promotion
- views or opinions on topical issues
- results of surveys or opinion polls
- customer stories/case studies
- deals/contracts
- new customers
- unusual applications
- new partnerships which have relevance for potential customers.

Remember, some publications are always looking for particular types of stories, e.g. product announcements, upgrades, job appointments, promotions, or financial results. Target the delivery of your press releases to make sure that those journalists and publications which definitely want your type, get it, using the method of delivery that they prefer.

** Be sure to accurately target your release according to journalist and publication, according to their audience. **

Content

All content has to:

- have a hook
- educate and inform

- entertain

- appeal to logic, sensation, emotion and belief

- differentiate between other releases and stories

- have credibility – substantiate your claims

- be localised – make sure the quotes are geographically appropriate for the journalist reading the release

- include differentiation – from all the other releases arriving on the journalist's desk that day. Differentiation comes from the product, its benefits, the company, its people, its services, its partners and its customers

- reinforce the company messages (see Chapter Four).

No press release can simply make wild, unsubstantiated claims – everything must be backed up with verifiable fact.

A press release is not an opportunity to tease. No journalist likes press releases which hint but don't tell, and withholding important information is more likely to ensure that the release is thrown away immediately.

Quotes

All press releases should contain at least one quote. Quotes:

- make a story come alive – a busy journalist writing a story may use a quote direct from the release without bothering to check the story

- can add depth

- give expert opinion or customer experience

- personalise a story

- should add gravitas

- can add humour

- can convey strong opinions which would look out of place in a straight narrative

- should be used to express opinion, and can start 'I think ...' or 'In my view ...'
- should not be trite comments, such as 'This product has changed my life.'

Quotes should appear on the front page of the press release, supporting the statements or news in the opening paragraphs.

- Use more than one sentence in the quote so that if several publications use it they may use different words by picking different sentences from the quote. If the same quote appears in several publications, the effect is diminished.
- Attribute the quote to someone senior and relevant to the topic of the press release.
- Give the commentator's/spokesperson's full job title.
- Make sure that the spokesperson is available for further comment if the journalist calls. The person quoted should be trained to be receptive and helpful, and must understand the journalist's agenda.
- The quote can be from a company representative, a customer or an independent expert.
- Quotes should not use indirect reported speech, such as 'Mr Jones said that the product will revolutionise the way that roads are built and people use them'. Better to say: '"The product will revolutionise the way roads are built and people use them," said Mr Jones.'

Expert opinion

Independent expert opinion is extremely valuable and carries significant weight.

- If a recognised and respected expert will say that your product is innovative, good value, or just plain interesting, you have newsworthy differential.
- Use the commendation near the top of the press release.
- Use the expert's view on other marketing material too.

■ Your objective is to make journalists want to talk to your expert, so make sure that they are prepared to talk to a journalist who calls. Get them trained in time.

** Some journalists use a specialist's name as the main hook for the story. That's fine. **

** There is nothing worse for a journalist or more embarrassing for the person promoting the product than if a journalist calls an expert whose name has been used in the press release, only to be met with a blank wall or negative response. Make sure that your expert is primed, trained, knows that they have been quoted and a journalist might call. **

Photographs

People remember pictures and faces more easily than they remember words and copy.

■ Editors choose stories according to the quality of the pictures.

■ Editors give better prominence to a story with a good picture.

■ Photographs should be lively, interesting and attention-grabbing.

■ Have a selection of black-and-white and colour shots.

■ Have some plain and straightforward and some unusual.

■ Always have shots prepared in advance of any meeting, event or interview.

■ All press packs should contain photographs.

■ Do not send photographs with every press release – many journalists, particularly freelances, throw them straight into the bin. Be selective, sending photographs to editors or others specifically wanting them. State at the end of the press release that photographs are available.

■ Provide landscape and portrait sized photographs.

■ Keep mug shots plain.

- Use a professional photographer – using an amateur is false economy.
- Don't use a high street photographer who usually does weddings. Use a press photographer to shoot the sort of pictures that will look good in print.
- Let the professional press photographer do it their way.
- Encourage the photographer to avoid the plain, bland photographs which usually accompany press releases.
- A good picture has an image which is sharp and unfunny.
- Have a selection of 'arty' shot, plain and formal, with a corporate logo or brand name, and without logo or company name in the background.

Make sure the photograph is labelled on the back:

- who or what is in the picture
- date of photograph
- the job title of the person
- contact phone number and email address
- the PR contact, with out-of-hours phone number and email address.

Alternatively, use an agency like PRshots to store your photographs and deliver them to the media in the right format at the right time (see *www.prshots.com*).

** If you have the company logo in the background of a picture, don't be surprised if it isn't used. **

When instructing a photographer, the cult of the personality means the subject's attitude and pose is important.

	Positive	Negative
A hand framing or supporting the face	Versatile Can convey a quizzical but assured image	Can look camp or arch
Gormless grin – aims to avoid glumness, sombre, over- serious attitude	Helps readers smile and hopefully warm to subject	Can look daft, especially on a serious story

continued	Positive	Negative
Classic serious star pose	High quality ensures regular requests for comments	Quickly dates with high circulation and use
Serious commentator, slight quirky smile	Pure image can be hard to sustain	Vulnerable to disaster and negative reaction from customers and press if image is tarnished
		Risk of disillusioning customers

Embargoes

Unless you are working for the government (which uses a D-notice system) don't use an embargo – they are meaningless. Embargoes are a request without any legal support or way of enforcement, not an instruction.

Some PRs use embargoes thinking:

- the journalist will be intrigued
- the embargo will be respected
- the embargo will ensure that the story is used simultaneously by all journalists.

All these assumptions are wrong.

- There is no legal enforcement for embargoes.
- Journalists often simply ignore them.
- Many journalists hate them.
- They indicate a naïve PR.

** By laying down an embargo you are trying to stop the journalist doing what comes naturally to them. **

What's the point of giving a news-hungry journalist a piece of news that they are not supposed to use?

<< Embargoes are strictly a request, not a right. >>

What are you going to do if the journalist ignores your embargo? If you have a story which is particularly sensitive and you don't want the information made available to the public before a certain date, then don't send it out. A journalist is under no obligation to recognise or respect the restrictions of an embargo.

When a journalist gets a press release

They will:

- scan the headline quickly
- if interested, scan the standfirst
- if interested, scan the first paragraph
- check who it is from
- check what it's about
- satisfy the 'So what?' factor
- bin it
- delete it
- file it
- print it out
- archive it
- save it
- use it
- call or email the PR or contact quoted.

The vast majority of press releases are not read, but press releases are still an essential element in any media campaign.

** The journalist will be irritated if they are forced to go through the PR to contact the company spokesperson – make contact as easy as possible for the journalist. **

In an editorial office, snail-mail press releases are often opened by one person (frequently the editorial assistant) who creates a large stack, which is passed around the whole office. Sending individual envelopes to each journalist is often a waste of time, but sending several copies of each release to each publication is often worthwhile, in case one journalist hangs on to the first.

Editorial offices have different policies on handling electronic press releases – check with each on their preferences.

Writing well

It goes without saying that your press release will be read by journalists – professional writers. Consequently, your release should be well written. Unfortunately, and surprisingly, many are not.

The press release must:

- have proper sentence construction
- have correct tenses throughout, with company names in singular ('The BBC has' not 'The BBC have')
- correct punctuation
- be written in an active, tight style or 'voice' by being direct and positive, and making definite assertions
- be concise but not abrupt. Too many short sentences are difficult to read, but long sentences fail to hold the reader's attention
- translate whatever you want to say into the simplest words
- flatter your readers by not talking down to them, but do not baffle them

- spell things out – don't assume that the journalist understands what you are talking about
- do not assume prior knowledge or experience of your company or product.

The press release must not use:

- typos or literals (spelling mistakes)
- repetition
- tame, colourless language
- clichés
- techie-speak
- jargon
- hyperbole
- euphemisms
- a dry, academic style or be written like an essay
- empty, meaningless phrases or 'weasel' words
- self-praise
- exaggeration
- unnecessary drama
- rhetoric, marketing puff and jargon particularly in quotes
- Gobbledegook.

Use your spell checker, and then double check it again. Get someone else to read it before you send it.

✹✹ If you are unsure of your writing ability, employ a professional to help. ✹✹

Press release writing is one of the services which professional PR agencies offer, and many freelance journalists will also write releases.

Refer to journalists' style books for writing guidance, such as Strunk and White's *The Elements of Style*. (Allyn & Bacon, USA, 1979).

For details of media training and courses on writing press releases, go to *www.anniegurton.com* or email *media.training@anniegurton.com*

Delivery

Press releases can be delivered to the target journalist:

- by post (snail mail)
- by email (see Chapter Seven on Computer-aided journalism, CAJ)
- by fax – almost obsolete
- by hand
- through news distribution agencies
- on CDs or disks, but not many journalists will put 'strange' CDs into their machines, so this is not a recommended method.

All press releases should be posted on your web site in your web press office as soon as possible.

- Make sure your database is accurate every time you use it – journalists move around so rapidly that staffers are often gone and job titles are changed. Inaccuracy does not help your credibility.
- Make sure every journalist gets the press releases they need, how and when they want them.

** Some PRs don't bother to send press releases to those journalists who request them by post. Little do they know that most journalists who request them by email simply delete them from their inbox. **

Press releases that fail

Surveys show that 95 per cent of press releases are thrown in the bin within 30 seconds of being opened, whether received by snail mail or email.

The most common reasons for press releases failing to interest a journalist are:

- headline confused
- no clear benefit to journalist's audience
- standfirst too wordy without explaining the story
- too technical
- too boring
- layout too dense – unable to grasp the story at a glance
- layout with too much white space – If the story isn't in the first half-page, forget it
- printed with single-line spacing and on both sides of the page
- introduction too wordy – get straight to the point
- no obvious angle or hook
- inspires the 'So what?' reaction
- old news.

** So many press releases are obviously just sent out to satisfy clients' demands, with no regard to what journalists want. **

PRs have to be prepared to tell clients to wait until they have some real news, or look harder for a story among the events within the company. Often customers give the best stories and PRs miss them.

<< A professional and competent PR will not hesitate to tell the client that their precious press release will be a waste of time, effort and money. Unfortunately, too many PRs go through the press release game just to satisfy the clients' expectations. The PRs should be training the clients in the realities of media life. >>

Journalists' codes
of practice

Journalists' code of practice

Drawn up by the Editors' Code Committee and published by The Press Complaints Commission (PCC).

To make a complaint or find out more about the PCC and its powers, visit *www.pcc.org.uk*

All members of the press have a duty to maintain the highest professional and ethical standards. This Code sets the benchmark for those standards. It both protects the rights of individuals and upholds the public's right to know.

The Code is the cornerstone of the system of self-regulation to which the industry has made a binding commitment. Editors and publishers must ensure that the Code is observed rigorously, not only by their staff but also by anyone who contributes to their publications.

It is essential to the workings of an agreed code that it be honoured not only to the letter but in the full spirit. The Code should not be interpreted so narrowly as to compromise its commitment to respect the rights of the individual, nor so broadly that it prevents publication in the public interest.

PCC Code

1 Accuracy
i) Newspapers and periodicals should take care not to publish inaccurate, misleading or distorted material, including pictures.
ii) Whenever it is recognised that a significant inaccuracy, misleading statement or distorted report has been published, it should be corrected promptly and with due prominence.
iii) An apology must be published whenever appropriate.
iv) Newspapers, whilst free to be partisan, must distinguish clearly between comment, conjecture and fact.
v) A newspaper or periodical must report fairly and accurately the outcome of an action for defamation to which it has been a party.

2 Opportunity to reply
A fair opportunity for reply to inaccuracies must be given to individuals or organisations when reasonably called for.

3 Privacy
i) Everyone is entitled to respect for his or her private and family life, home, health and correspondence. A publication will be expected to justify intrusions into any individual's private life without consent.
ii) The use of long-lens photography to take pictures of people in private places without their consent is unacceptable.

Note: Private places are public or private property where there is a reasonable expectation of privacy.

4 Harassment

i)   Journalists and photographers must neither obtain nor seek to obtain information or pictures through intimidation, harassment or persistent pursuit.

ii) They must not photograph individuals in private places (as defined by the note to clause 3) without their consent; must not persist in telephoning, questioning, pursuing or photographing individuals after having been asked to desist; must not remain on their property after having been asked to leave, and must not follow them.

iii) Editors must ensure that those working for them comply with these requirements and must not publish material from other sources which does not meet these requirements.

5 Intrusion into grief or shock

In cases involving personal grief or shock, enquiries should be carried out and approaches made with sympathy and discretion. Publication must be handled sensitively at such times but this should not be interpreted as restricting the right to report judicial proceedings.

6 Children

i)   Young people should be free to complete their time at school without unnecessary intrusion.

ii) Journalists must not interview or photograph a child under the age of 16 on subjects involving the welfare of the child or any other child in the absence of or without the consent of a parent or other adult who is responsible for the children.

iii) Pupils must not be approached or photographed while at school without the permission of the school authorities.

iv) There must be no payment to minors for material involving the welfare of children nor payments to parents or guardians for material about their children or wards unless it is demonstrably in the child's interest.

v)   Where material about the private life of a child is published, there must be justification for publication other than the fame, notoriety or position of his or her parents or guardian.

7 **Children in sex cases**

1. The press must not, even where the law does not prohibit it, identify children under the age of 16 who are involved in cases concerning sexual offences, whether as victims or as witnesses.

2. In any press report of a case involving a sexual offence against a child.

    i)   The child must not be identified.

    ii) The adult may be identified.

    iii) The word 'incest' must not be used where a child victim might be identified.

    iv) Care must be taken that nothing in the report implies the relationship between the accused and the child.

8 **Listening devices**

Journalists must not obtain or publish material obtained by using clandestine listening devices or by intercepting private telephone conversations.

9 **Hospitals**

i)   Journalists or photographers making enquiries at hospitals or similar institutions should identify themselves to a responsible executive and obtain permission before entering non-public areas.

ii) The restrictions on intruding into privacy are particularly relevant to enquiries about individuals in hospitals or similar institutions.

10 **Reporting of crime.**

i)   The press must avoid identifying relatives or friends of persons convicted or accused of crime without their consent.

ii) Particular regard should be paid to the potentially vulnerable position of children who are witnesses to, or victims of, crime. This should not be interpreted as restricting the right to report judicial proceedings.

11 **Misrepresentation**

i)   Journalists must not generally obtain or seek to obtain information or pictures through misrepresentation or subterfuge.

ii) Documents or photographs should be removed only with the consent of the owner.

iii) Subterfuge can be justified only in the public interest and only when material cannot be obtained by any other means.

12 Victims of sexual assault

The press must not identify victims of sexual assault or publish material likely to contribute to such identification unless there is adequate justification and, by law, they are free to do so.

13 Discrimination

i) The press must avoid prejudicial or pejorative reference to a person's race, colour, religion, sex or sexual orientation or to any physical or mental illness or disability.

ii) It must avoid publishing details of a person's race, colour, religion, sexual orientation, physical or mental illness or disability unless these are directly relevant to the story.

14 Financial journalism

i) Even where the law does not prohibit it, journalists must not use for their own profit financial information they receive in advance of its general publication, nor should they pass such information to others.

ii) They must not write about shares or securities in whose performance they know that they or their close families have a significant financial interest without disclosing the interest to the editor or financial editor.

iii) They must not buy or sell, either directly or through nominees or agents, shares or securities about which they have written recently or about which they intend to write in the near future.

15 Confidential sources

Journalists have a moral obligation to protect confidential sources of information.

16 Payment for articles

i) Payment or offers of payment for stories or information must not be made directly or through agents to witnesses or potential witnesses in current criminal proceedings except where the material concerned ought to be published in the public interest and there is an overriding need to make or promise to make a payment for this to be done. Journalists must take every possible step to ensure that no financial dealings have influence on the evidence that those witnesses may give.

(An editor authorising such a payment must be prepared to demonstrate that there is a legitimate public interest at stake involving matters that the public has a right to know. The payment or, where accepted, the offer of payment to any witness who is actually cited to give evidence should be disclosed to the prosecution and the defence and the witness should be advised of this.)

ii) Payment or offers of payment for stories, pictures or information must not be made directly or through agents to convicted or confessed criminals or to their associates – who may include family, friends and colleagues – except where the material concerned ought to be published in the public interest and payment is necessary for this to be done.

There may be exceptions to some clauses where they can be demonstrated to be in the public interest.

1. The public interest includes:
    i) Detecting or exposing crime or a serious misdemeanour.
    ii) Protecting public health and safety.
    iii) Preventing the public from being misled by some statement or action of an individual or organisation.
2. In any case where the public interest is invoked, the Press Complaints Commission will require a full explanation by the editor demonstrating how the public interest was served.

3. There is a public interest in freedom of expression itself. The Commission will therefore have regard to the extent to which material has, or is about to, become available to the public.

4. In cases involving children, editors must demonstrate an exceptional public interest to override the normally paramount interest of the child

Journalists' Code of Conduct

Published by the National Union of Journalists (NUJ).

1. A journalist has a duty to maintain the highest professional and ethical standards.

2. A journalist shall at all times defend the principle of the freedom of the press and other media in relation to the collection of information and the expression of comment and criticism. He/she shall strive to eliminate distortion, news suppression and censorship.

3. A journalist shall strive to ensure that the information he/she disseminates is fair and accurate, avoid the expression of comment and conjecture as a well-established fact and falsification by distortion, selection or misrepresentation.

4. A journalist shall rectify promptly any harmful inaccuracies, ensure that correction and apologies receive due prominence and afford the right of reply to persons criticised when the issue is of sufficient importance.

5. A journalist shall obtain information, photographs and illustrations only by straightforward means. The use of other means can only be justified by overriding considerations of the public interest. The journalist is entitled to exercise a personal conscientious objection to the use of such means.

6. Subject to the justification by overriding considerations of the public interest, a journalist shall do nothing which entails intrusion into grief and distress.

7. A journalist shall protect confidential sources of information.

8. A journalist shall not accept bribes, nor shall he/she allow other inducements to influence the performance of his/her professional duties.

9. A journalist shall not lend him/herself to the distortion or suppression of the truth because of advertising or other considerations.

10. A journalist shall only mention a person's age, race, colour, creed, illegitimacy, disability, marital status, gender or sexual orientation if this information is strictly relevant. A journalist shall neither originate nor process material which encourages discrimination, ridicule, prejudice or hatred on any of the above-mentioned grounds.

11. A journalist shall not take private advantage of information gained in the course of his/her duties, before the information is public knowledge.

12. A journalist shall not by way of statement, voice or appearance endorse by advertisement any commercial product or service save for the promotion of his/her own work or of the medium by which he/she is employed.

The Broadcasting Standards Commission

The Commission has a brief to regulate and watch all UK media and ensure that content and journalistic standards are maintained. It considers and adjudicates complaints and monitors, reports to the government on standards and fairness, and researches and reports on journalistic activity.

For information or to complain, contact   020 7808 1000 *www.bsc.org.uk* *bsc@bsc.org.uk*

5

Agencies

Here we give an independent cross-section of PR, marketing and media strategy agencies for those wanting to hire an external professional service.

There are thousands of PR agencies in the UK and this is a random selection. They vary dramatically according to size, speciality, services, experience and competence. **Inclusion in this listing is not a recommendation and is not intended as approval or accreditation**. All information is as supplied by the agencies. You are advised to follow the guidelines set out in Chapter 10 for selecting an agency, or contact the Institute of Public Relations for other names or guidance on selection (020 7253 5151 *www.ipr.org.uk*).

APR Communications
London
Tel: 020 7937 7733   *www.aprcom.co.uk*

Beehive Marketing
Reading, Berks
Tel: 0118 988 9090   *www.beehivemarketing.com*

Berkeley PR
West London/Reading – Silicon Valley
Tel: 0118 988 2992   *www.berkeleypr.co.uk*

Biss Lancaster
London
Tel: 020 7497 3001   *www.bisslancaster.com*

Bite Communications
London
Tel: 020 8741 1123   *www.bitecomm.co.uk*

Bluegrass
Andover, Hants
Tel: 01264 323141   *www.bluegrass.co.uk*

Brodeur APlus Group
Slough, Berks
Tel: 01753 790700   *www.brodeuruk.com*

BSMG Worldwide
London
Tel: 020 7841 5555 *www.bsmg.co.uk*

Buffalo Communications
London
Tel: 020 7292 8680   *www.buffalo.co.uk*

Burston Marsteller
London
Tel: 020 7831 6262   *www.bm.com*

Charlwood House PR
Tel: 020 8878 8871 *www.charlwoodhouse.com*

CHC
Keighley, West Yorks
Tel: 01535 637055 *www.chc-pr.co.uk*

Citigate
London
Tel: 020 7282 8000 *www.citigate.com*

Click Information Terminology (Click IT)
Odiham, Hants
Tel: 01428 647000 *www.click.co.uk*

Cohn & Wolfe
London
Tel: 020 7331 5300 *www.cohnwolfe.com*

DPA
Guildford, Surrey
Tel: 01483 414000 *www.dpacoms.com*

Eclat Marketing
Marlow, Bucks
Tel: 01628 400 900 *www.eclat.co.uk*

Edelman
London
Tel: 020 7344 1200 *www.edelman.com*

Eric Leach Marketing
Hounslow, Middlesex
Tel: 020 8758 7587 *www.ericleach.com*

Evus
London
Tel: 020 7386 9242   *www.evux.com*

Firefly Communications
London
Tel: 020 7381 4505   *www.firefly.co.uk*

Flameboy PR
Ascot, Berkshire
Tel: 01344 871 980   *www.flame-boy.co.uk*

Flapjack Communications
London
Tel: 020 7224 4554   *www.flapjack.com*

Ford-Peacock Consultancy
Hook Norton, Oxfordshire
Tel: 01608 730 565   *www.ford-peacock.com*

Freud Communications
London
Tel: 020 7580 2626   *www.freudcommunications.com*

GCI Group
London
Tel: 020 7351 2400   *www.gciuk.com*

Goode International
Reading, Berkshire
Tel: 01491 873 323   *www.goodeint.com*

Grant Butler Coomber
Richmond, Surrey
Tel: 020 8322 1922   *www.grantbutlercoomber.com*

Harvard Public Relations
Harmondsworth, Middlesex
Tel: 020 8759 0005   *www.harvard.co.uk*

Herald Communications
London
Tel: 0207 340 6 300   *www.heraldcommunications.com*

Hill & Knowlton
London
Tel: 020 7133 000   *www.hillandknowlton.com*

Hobsbawm Macauley Communications (HMC)
London
Tel: 020 7612 1555   *www.forwardplanning.net*

Insight Group
Slough, Berkshire
Tel: 01344 871 900   *www.insightgroup.co.uk*

Insight Marketing
Macclesfield, Cheshire
Tel: 01625 500800   *www.insightmkt.com*

The ITPR Partnership
Chertsey, Surrey
Tel: 01932 578800   *www.itpr.co.uk*

Joslin Shaw PR
London
Tel: 020 7226 9177   *www.joshaw.co.uk*

Kaizo
London
Tel: 020 7850 8852   *www.kaizo.net*

Key Communications
London
Tel: 020 7580 0222   *www.keycommunications.co.uk*

Kinross & Render
London
Tel: 020 7592 3100   *www.kinross-and-render.co.uk*

Lesniak Jones Liddell (LJL)
Newcastle under Lyme, Staffordshire, Bourne End, Bucks
Tel: 01628 522222   *www.ljl.co.uk*

Lewis
London
Tel: 020 7802 2626   *www.lewispr.com*

Lighthouse
London
Tel: 020 7236 0960   *www.lighthousepr.com*

Lindsay Brown Associates
London
Tel: 020 7490 1030   *www.lbapr.com*

Livewire PR
London
Tel: 020 8547 3418   *www.livewirepr.com*

Marbles
Henley-on-Thames, Oxfordshire
Tel: 01491 411789   *www.marbles.co.uk*

MCC International
Hampshire
Tel: 01962 888 100   *www.mccint.com*

Media Link
Pangbourne, Berkshire
Tel: 0118 984 3386   *www.medialink.co.uk*

MMD
Old Isleworth, Middlesex
Tel: 020 8380 4901   *www.mmd-marcoms.co.uk*

Mulberry Marketing Communications
London
Tel: 020 7928 7676   *www.mulberrymc.com*

Multimedia Public Relations & Marketing
Chepstow, Monmouthshire
Tel: 01291 626 200   *www.multimediapr.com*

Noiseworks
Maidenhead, Berkshire
Tel: 01628 628080   *www.noiseworks.com*

Oast Communications
Westerham, Kent
Tel: 01959 568 500   *www.oastcommunications.com*

Opus Group
Basingstoke, Berks
Tel: 01256 399 800   *www.opusgroup.co.uk*

Profile
Richmond, Surrey
Tel: 020 8948 6611   *www.profilepr.co.uk*

PRPR
Hemel Hempstead, Herts
Tel: 01442 245030   *www.prpr.co.uk*

Portfolio Communications
London
Tel: 020 7240 6959   *www.portmet.co.uk*

Premier Marketing Services
Kenley, Surrey
Tel: 020 8660 3152   *www.charlwoodhouse.com*

The Right Image
Walton-on-Thames, Surrey
Tel 01932 240 055   *www.therightimage.co.uk*

Spark Communications
London
Tel: 020 7202 8490   *www.sparkcomms.co.uk*

Spreckley Partners
London
Tel: 020 7388 9988   *www.spreckley.co.uk*

Strategic PR
Old Amersham, Bucks
Tel: 01494 434434   *www.strategicpr.net*

Two One Communications
Salisbury, Wiltshire
Tel: 01722 340 352   *www.two-one.co.uk*

Wildfire
Hampton Wick, Surrey
Tel: 020 8255 6603   *www.wildfire.co.uk*

Media training

For business and IT industry media training contact:
media.training@anniegurton.com or visit *www.anniegurtonmediatraining.com*

appendix 6

Glossary of terms

Advertorial

At first glance it sometimes looks like genuine editorial journalism but in fact advertorial is a version of advertising. While pure journalism contains a balance of views and opinions, advertorial contains only views which are positive and have been paid for.

Banner

A big, wide headline, or the title of a publication, as in 'banner headline'.

Bleed

Technique of making the editorial or advertising run right to the edge of the page, rather than leaving a narrow border.

Blurb

Marketing or PR copy, or information about a product sent by a PR company.

Body copy
Main text of a feature or story.

Box-out
A box within a feature containing a particular editorial, a short story or a case study.

Broadsheet
Large-sized newspaper. General term to mean the quality press, as opposed to the tabloids.

Bulletin
A short radio or television news item or programme.

Byline
The attribution of an article to a specific journalist: 'By John Smith' or 'by Sarah Jones'.

Camera-ready copy (CRC)
An image or page ready to be transferred direct to the printing process.

Caption
The short sentence under a photograph which explains who or what it depicts.

Case
In old print rooms, the capital letters were kept in the higher tray and the small letters kept in a lower tray, hence 'upper case' and 'lower case'.

Case study
A 'story' about a customer using your product or service.

Casting off
A near obsolete term for a task made almost unnecessary by new technology. In the old days, a journalist and sub-editor had to make sure their copy would fit the space allocated by working out how many words were required to fit a given space. A piece was then 'cast off' by being pruned to the right length. The

term comes from a old printing expression meaning to cast a line of metal type to fit an exact space. Most stories have to be cut to fit, but these days casting off is done easily on screen.

Catchline

Keyword usually at the top outside corner of a page which indicates what is on that page, such as 'News', 'Feature', 'Letters', and so forth. Helps the reader find their way around the publication.

Classified

Small advertisement.

Colour separation

A revenue stream for publishers – a scam involving charges for 'colour separation' in which editorial and media sales teams claim that editorial costs have to be paid by PR. Avoid publications which resort to low strategies like this.

Copy

The words produced by journalists. Refers to the written word.

Copy flow

The route or process that the copy follows from journalist to page or broadcast. Also refers to the electronic flowing in of text to a page at the layout stage.

Copy taster

The link on the editorial team of newspapers between the journalists and the sub-editors. Reads every story submitted and selects those to be used. On small titles, this task is usually performed by the editor.

Correspondent

A journalist covering a specific geographical or vertical market area.

Cover flash

A strip across the corner of a cover, or a bold star imposed on the top of the cover image, containing words which tell the reader that there is something special inside this issue. Can be used to indicate a sponsored competition or special offer or a particularly important story.

Crop

To trim or cut photographs in such a way that the best parts are emphasised and unwanted parts are not printed.

Cross-head

Short sentence or one word set in bold and larger type in the text of a feature or news story, which indicates to the reader something interesting coming up. Intended to retain the reader's attention, or to catch the eye of someone casually scanning the pages. Sometimes taken straight from the body copy (also known as a pull quote – pulled from the text), or sometimes written specially for the purpose, like a headline.

Deadline

The absolute date or hour when a journalist has to deliver copy. After this time only a major crisis would warrant changing anything – and even then it is sometimes not possible. Some journalists give false deadlines to encourage spokespeople to respond fast. Even if you suspect that you are being told false deadlines you have to behave as though that is the absolute cut-off point. Only ignore deadlines if you aim to deliver as quickly as possible.

Defamation

Unfair or injurious comment.

Display

Large advertisement.

D-notice

Defence advisory notice – a government request to journalists not to use information which would risk national security. For full details see *www.dnotice.org.uk*

DPS

Double-page spread. A feature which is spread across two facing pages.

Drop quote

Like a pull quote, a quotation copied from the text and run large to enhance the page design.

Dub

Copy a recording from one tape to another.

Editing

Amending and checking copy and tapes.

Editor

The most senior person on the editorial team, responsible to a publisher or producer. Legally responsible for all the contents.

Em

The basic measurement of width in newspaper layouts. Normally one-sixth of an inch (the 12-point em).

Embargo

Request to wait to publish or broadcast a story until a specific date or time. Not legally enforceable. See also D-notice.

En

Half an em.

Exclusive

A story that no other publication or programme has.

Extranet

Secure network linking customers, suppliers, partners and anyone else who is authorised to join a closed network, using the internet as the backbone.

Feature

A story that is not a news story and includes analysis.

Filler

A short story, usually at the bottom of a page or column.

Flannel panel
List of staff on the publication, sometimes with their contact details. Usually includes sales and production staff and the publishers, as well as the editorial team.

Flatplan
Visual schematic of the contents of a magazine or newspaper, showing which pages are for advertising and which are editorial.

Folio
Has several meanings but usually refers to the page number or a page of copy.

Freelance
A journalist who is self-employed, usually working for several publications or programmes.

Gatefold
A page which folds out, usually to carry advertising.

Gutter
The join in the middle of two facing pages.

Headline
The short, snappy title to a story or feature. Usually written by the sub-editors, not by the journalist who writes the copy.

House style
A standardised set of rules for spelling, punctuation and handling of copy adopted by each magazine or newspaper to achieve consistency. Serves to standardise the text, with the same titles or captions always being handled in the same way, and gives the unique character to the publication. Essential when copy is written by many contributors or there are several or changing sub-editors.

HyperText
The clickable links that connect web sites and auto-send emails.

Inside back
The page on the inside of the back cover.

Intranet

Internal communications system which uses the internet as a backbone.

Intro

Another name for the standfirst, or the two or three lines at the beginning of a story which come after the headline.

Kern

The space between letters and words. In word-processing software, kerning is automatic.

Layout

The design of an editorial page.

Leader

A statement of views or mission statement. Positions the magazine or newspaper in the eyes of its readership and advertisers.

Lineage

Small unboxed advertisement.

Literal

A typing mistake, or 'typo'.

Masthead

The paper's name and the standfirst running under it, which explicitly declares its target audience or the aim of the magazine or newspaper.

MetaTag

Hidden HTML words and codes used by search engines to find web sites. By using key MetaTags, you can ensure that your site is located by search engines.

Morgue

Press cutting library or holding of back issues.

NIB

A nib is a News In Brief item in a newspaper or magazine, usually less than 100 words.

Orphan

A single line at the bottom of a page which is the first line of the next paragraph, continued on the next page. Good subbing will remove all widows and orphans.

Overmatter

Wording in excess of the space allocated. The sub-editor will cut out the over-matter to make the piece fit.

Pagination

The number of pages in the publication. Split between editorial and advertising.

Perfect bound

When a magazine is bound together with glue at the spine and each page is separate. The alternative is stapled.

Pix

Pictures or photographs.

Point size

The size of type. One point is approximately 1/72 inch.

Press day

The day that a publication closes and goes to the printers. The last day for news. Everyone in the editorial department will be very busy. Not a good day to telephone.

Press pack

Collection of press releases, photographs, product specifications and information given to journalists, especially at events, conferences or seminars.

Producer

Person responsible for putting a programme on air.

Publisher

The person who appoints the editor of a magazine or newspaper, and sets the pagination, yield and budgets on each issue. In law, the editor is more powerful. In practice, the publisher has ultimate power, but a strong editor will resist the publisher's attempts to influence and control.

Pull quote

A quote which is selected by the sub-editor and reprinted in a larger typeface, as part of the layout and design of a page.

Red Top

The tabloid newspapers, many of which use a red tint behind the title.

Reporter

A journalist, usually working on news stories. The person responsible for compiling and writing (and, on TV and radio, presenting) the piece.

Running head

A running headline on each page of a feature, usually on the outside corner of the page, so a reader can flick through and see at a glance where the feature is located and what it's about.

Script

Broadcast journalist's copy.

Sic

A Latin word used by editors to indicate an apparent mis-spelling or doubtful word in a quote, to indicate that the editor is not responsible for the fault and to lay the blame on the source being quoted.

Sidebar

Short story run within a feature, often based on a case study. Or the sidebar can be a column on a layout dedicated to short stories.

Side-head

Another name for a cross-head, or a short caption which appears in the middle of a news story or feature. Often put in by the page designer as a visual to make the page more interesting. Written by the sub.

Slug

A short caption which usually goes across the top of a page, either to highlight its content or to point out that it is advertorial.

Sound bite

Short comment extracted from an interview to illustrate a report. Usually 7–40 seconds.

Spam

Junk email.

Spike

To 'spike' a story is literally to impale it on a spike of rejections. To reject.

Standfirst

The caption which goes under a headline or title, to give a little more information about it. So, for example, you may have a headline which reads, 'BBC in uproar' and the standfirst will tell you a little more about it: 'Journalists threaten strike because of cut in expenses.' Or the title of a publication may be 'Autocomputer' and the standfirst will be 'For users of automatic computers in industry'.

Stet

An editing term, taken from the Latin and meaning 'let it stand', cancelling a deletion or other change previously made on a page proof.

Story

A potential news item or article which has to be made to 'stand up'.

Strapline

The line underneath the title of a publication which explains who the reader is supposed to be, and at whom the contents are aimed. So, *PC Dealer* is 'The weekly newspaper for computer resellers'. Also used to refer to the catchline on the outside corner of a page to indicate the contents.

Style sheet

Several pages, or a small booklet, which define how the publication handles specific types of copy, such as spellings of job titles and names, the way pictures are captioned, etc. A detailed definition and description of a publication's style, which means that if a sub-editor gets run over by a bus, someone else can take over without any impact on the look and feel of the title. Prescribes accepted abbreviations, contractions and spellings. Should be updated regularly to reflect the changing use of language.

Sub-editor

The person on a publication who:

- checks facts, names and places
- checks and puts right errors in grammar and spelling
- ensures that the style of the copy matches the style sheet
- cuts the text to fit the space allocated
- combines material from several sources to make a composite story
- rewrites part or all of the copy, if necessary, to achieve the right balance and style
- checks that the story is accurate and legally safe
- gives the right instructions to the production editor and printers to ensure the page looks right as it should
- revises a story, if necessary, for later editions
- writes captions, headlines, standfirsts, cross-heads
- selects pull quotes and drop quotes from text
- makes sure the editorial copy is ready for deadline.

Tabloid

A small newspaper with pages half the size of a broadsheet. A general derogatory term meaning the down-market press.

Text

The main printed material.

Trade names

Registered trade names should be used with care, and always with a capital letter. It is better if possible to use the generic equivalent, for example:

- Hoover (vacuum cleaner)
- Sellotape (sticky tape)
- Elastoplast (sticky plaster)
- Coke/Coca-Cola (cola)
- Fibreglass (glass fibre).

If in doubt, contact the Institute of Trade Mark Agents (020 8686 2052).

Typo

A spelling mistake, particularly one made at the keying-in stage, or blamed on the typist.

URL

Uniform Resource Locator – the web address.

Web offset

A printing process.

Widow

A single word on a line, at the end of a paragraph. Sometimes a single word at the top left corner of a page, when the previous page's copy runs over. Good subbing will remove all widows and orphans.

WOB

White on black – a block of text reversed so that white type appears on a black background.

Index

accuracy of articles 308
advance briefings 83–4
advertising 56, 84–5
  relationship with editorials 87–9,
    139–40, 271–4
  threats to withdraw 88
advertorials 85–6, 327
agencies 252–60
  changing 253
  contact information 317–24
  effectiveness measurement 259–64
  journalists as clients 253
  journalists' view of 250–1, 269
  media evaluation services 263–4
  meeting the staff 253
  selecting 253, 256–8
  services offered 253–6
  working with 116–17, 258–9
all expenses-paid trips 78–9, 275
all-in effectiveness measurements 262
ambition of journalists 6
art editors 20
attitude/behaviour of journalists 9–12,
    120–1, 138
attribution of comments 183–4

background information 37
bad publicity 234–5
Banks, Kate 116–17
banner headlines 327
Barnes, Roger 246–7
BBC 162
behaviour/attitude of journalists 9–12,
    120–1, 138
Black, Luke 188–9

Blank, Jan 245–6
bleed 327
blurb 327
body copy 328
body language 178
Boston Matrix 112
box-out 328
brands 30
  brand awareness 262
  brand reputation 233–4
Branson, Sir Richard 42
bribes 135–6
Bridge Burners 10
broadcast editors 20
Broadcasting Standards Commission
    314
broadsheet newspapers 328
Brown, Rita 50
budgets 260–1
bulletins 328
buying editorial coverage 85, 312–13
bylines 328

camera-ready copy (CRC) 328
captions 328
case 328
case studies 57–8, 91–2, 328
  contacting journalists 23–4
  emails 266
  expectations of customers 188–9
  freelance journalists 189–90, 246–7
  commissioning 94
  internet publications 230
  journalists' working practices 267
  media training 115–16

press conferences 50, 147–8
press days 148–9
product reviews 93
relationships with journalists 245–6
reputation management 215–16
as a sales tool 57–8, 91–2
sub-editors 216–17
work experience students 229
working with PRs 116–17
casting off 328–9
catchlines 329
children 309–10
classified advertising 329
Code of Conduct 313–14
Code of Practice 307–13
    accuracy of articles 308
    and children 309–10
    confidentiality of sources 311
    crime reporting 310
    discrimination 311
    financial journalism 311
    harassment 309
    hospital enquiries 310
    intrusion 309
    listening devices 310
    misrepresentation 310–11
    opportunity to reply 308
    payment for articles 312–13
    privacy 308
    sex cases 310, 311
cold calling 80, 120, 122
colour separation 87, 89, 329
column inches measurement 262
commenting on competitors 173–5, 224
company web sites 205–8

comparisons of products 55–6
competition between journalists 82–4
competitions for readers 59–60, 226
competitors, commenting on 173–5, 224
complaints to editorial teams 236–7,
    240–1
computer-aided journalism 193–217
    e-invites 204–5
    online research 212–13
    press audits 202–3
    press monitoring services 212
    press release distribution 200–2
    virtual press conferences 208–9
    see also email; internet; web sites
confidentiality of sources 272, 311
contacting journalists 23–4, 120–49,
    219–20
    as an advertiser 139–40
    attitude of journalists 9–12, 120–1,
        138
    cold calling 80, 120, 122
    databases of journalists 29, 81, 120,
        245–6
    and deadlines 140–2, 148–9
    by email 80, 126–7, 266
    by fax 81, 129
    and features lists 138–40
    gifts and freebies 135–6, 272, 273–4,
        276, 277
    hooking a journalist's attention
        33–40, 133–4, 294
    offering exclusives 134
    personal contact 3, 80–1
    and personal relationships 143–5,
        219–20, 245–6, 250–1

personal visits 129–30
pitching story ideas 130–4
by post 80, 128
preparation and research 120–2
seniority and numbers of contacts
    122–5
and stunts 136–7, 277
and teaser campaigns 136–7, 271
by telephone 80, 127
voicemail 128–9
by web sites 81, 205–10
see also meeting journalists
content of press releases 294–5
contributed articles 58
controversial stories/views 9, 35–6
copy 329
copy approval 185, 277
copy flow 329
copy taster 329
copyright laws 22
correspondents 329
costs of media training 46
cover flash 329
crib sheets 112–13
crime reporting 310
crop 330
cross-head 330
cue cards 112–13
customer hospitality 79–80

D-notice 299, 330
daily publications, deadlines 141
damage limitation 233–47
  bad publicity 234–5
  complaints to editorial teams 236–7,
    240–1

honest approach 236
and the internet 239–40
libel actions 241, 243–4
Press Complaints Commission 241,
    242, 307
speed and efficiency 235–6
what not to do 238–9
what to do 235–8
databases of journalists 29, 81, 120,
    245–6
Davies, Paul 23
deadlines 39, 140–2, 148–9, 330
defamation 330
desk research 32
directors 19
discrimination 311
display adverts 330
distribution of press releases 200–3,
    271, 273, 303
double-page spread 330
dress code 64, 179
drop quote 331
dubbing 331

e-invites 204–5
editing 331
editorial coverage 2, 3, 84–92, 269
  accuracy of 308
  buying 85, 312–13
  colour separation costs 87, 89
  compared to advertising 3
  copy approval 185, 277
  feature stories 17–18, 34
  news stories 17, 34
  opinion pages 57, 89–91, 225

presenting product information 7–8
relationship with advertising 87–9,
    139–40, 271–2, 273–4
right of reply 240, 242, 308
editorial freedom 5, 88
editors 30, 123, 331
  art editors 20
  broadcast 20
  entertaining 77–8, 276
  letters to 59
  print 19–20
  production 20
  reviews editors 56
  role of 5, 123
  sub-editors 20, 124, 216–17, 337
Editors' Code Committee 307
effectiveness measurement 259–64
electronic press audits 202–3
electronic press release distribution
    200–2
electronic press services 202
electronic publications 211, 230
  deadlines 141
Ellison, Larry 42
em 331
email
  contacting journalists by 80, 126–7,
    266
  e-invites 204–5
  interviews by 51, 159, 198–200
  and press audits 204
  responding to 207
  uses of 196
embargoes 66, 270, 299–300, 331
en 331

ending an interview 173
enquiries from the press 227–8
entertaining 77–8, 276
evaluation of messages 259–64
events 3, 79–80
  and press days 148–9
exclusive stories 134, 331
exhibitions 73–5
expectations of customers 188–9
expenses-paid trips 78–9, 275
expert opinion 296–7
extranets 208, 331

FAB (Facts, Advantages, Benefits) 105
face to face interviews see interviews
facilities visits 75
factory visits 75
facts and statistics 34–5, 100–5
failed press releases 304
faxing journalists 81, 129
feature stories 17–18, 34, 331
feature writers 18–19
features lists 138–40, 202
FeaturesExec 202
Ferrets 10
fillers 331
financial journalism 311
flannel panel 332
flatpan 332
Fledglings 10–11
folio 332
following up 219–30
  by journalists 227–8
  keeping stories alive 226–7
  press conferences 222

press releases 220–2, 270
forums 210
free trips 78–9, 275
freebies 135–6, 272, 273–4, 276, 277
freelance journalists 14, 15–16, 123,
    274, 332
  case studies 94, 189–90, 246–7
  commissioning freelance writers 94
  writing advertorials 86
  writing opinion copy 90
frequency of publication 21, 141
Frost, Sir David 161

gatefold 332
Gates, Bill 41
gifts and freebies 135–6, 272, 273–4,
    276, 277
gimmicks 136–7, 277
Green Room hospitality 176
gutter 332

Haji-Ioannou, Stelios 42
harassment 309
Harvey Jones, Sir John 41
headlines 34, 332
hooking a journalist's attention 33–40,
    133–4, 294
hospital enquiries 310
house style 332
Humphreys, John 161
HyperText 332

identifying stories 29–30
in-house distribution of press releases
    202–3

in-house PR departments 262
influence of journalists 2–3
Ingram, Suzie 50–1
inside back 332
internet 12, 14, 193–8
  crisis management strategy 239–40
  online research 212–13
  press monitoring services 212
  voice-over-internet (VoIP) technology
      198
  see also computer-aided journalism;
      web sites
internet publications 211, 230
  deadlines 141
interviews 151–90
  annoying/flustering interviewees 164
  answering questions 172
  attribution of comments 183–4
  avoiding questions 167
  check lists 155–7
  commenting on competitors 173–5,
      224
  email interviews 51, 159, 198–200
  ending an interview 173
  face to face 158
  journalists' style 160–2, 163–73
  need for 151–3
  and nervousness 153
  No Comment responses 154, 155,
      185
  on and off the record 181–3
  preconceived views 170, 171
  preparation 98–9, 155–7, 170–1
  questioning techniques 163, 167, 172
    hostile questions 175–6

questions not to ask 184–6
radio interviews 176–80
recorded conversations 8–9
refusing 153–5
starting an interview 168
successful interviewees 165–8, 184–6
telephone interviews 51, 57, 158,
    160, 169
television interviews 176–80
thanking journalists 184–5, 224, 275
types of 158–60
unexpected requests for 168–73
see also meeting journalists
intranets 208, 333
intro 333
intrusion into grief or shock 309
irrelevant comments/information 142–3

jargon 132–3
job specifications 19–21
job titles 19–21
Jones, Jane 215–16
journalists
    attitude/behaviour of 9–12, 120–1,
        138
    personal relationships with 143–5,
        219–20, 245–6, 250–1
    self-image of 4
    stereotypes of 6
    web sites 209–10
    working practices 8–9, 267
Journalist's Code of Practice 10

kern 333
Kiam, Victor 41

layout 333
leaders 333
letters pages 59, 225, 226
letters to journalists 80, 128
libel actions 241, 243–4
life cycle of products 111–12
lineage 333
listening devices 310
literal 333
litigation 241, 243–4
lunches/meals 77–8, 276

masthead 333
meals 77–8, 276
measuring effectiveness 259–64
media evaluation services 263–4
media personalities 41–5
media plans
    hooking a journalist's attention
        33–40, 133–4, 294
    measuring effectiveness of 259–64
    objectives of 27
    research 31–3
    target audiences 5, 28–31, 36–7, 292
media service websites 196–7
media tours 76–7
media training 45–8, 115–16, 324
    costs 46
    subjects of case studies 92
mediadisk.co.uk 197
meeting journalists
    customer hospitality 79–80
    events 79–80
        and press days 148–9
    exhibitions 73–5

expenses-paid trips 78–9, 275
facilities visits 75
lunches/meals 77–8
media tours 76–7
one-to-one meetings 69–71, 76
press conferences see press
    conferences
press receptions 67–9, 74
  and unforeseen events 147–8
seminars 72–3
show stands 73–5
workshops 72–3
see also contacting journalists
message development 30, 97–117
  anticipating questions 108–11
  check lists 157
  crib sheets 112–13
  cue cards 112–13
  evaluation of messages 259–64
  evolving 111–12
  FAB (Facts, Advantages, Benefits)
      105
  facts and statistics 34–5, 100–5
  hooking a journalist's attention
      33–40, 133–4, 294
  identifying issues and topics 106–7
  media messages 105
  preparing for meetings/interviews
      98–9, 155–7, 170–1
  and product life cycles 111–12
  sales messages 105
  testimonials 105
  writing styles 99–100, 290–2, 301–3
MetaTag 333
Miles, Sarah 24

Millennium Dome 2–3
misquotes 4, 21
misrepresentation 310–11
mobile broadcasts 179–80
monthly publications, deadlines 141
Moore, Susannah 115–16
morgue 333
mutual needs of journalists/managers 7

National Union of Journalists (NUJ)
    313–14
Newman, Eddie 147–8
news journalists 18
news stories 17, 34
news web sites 210–12
NIB (News In Brief) 333
No Comment responses 154, 155, 185
non-disclosure agreements (NDAs)
    66–7
numbers of contacts 122–5

on and off the record 181–3
one-to-one meetings 69–71, 76
online research 212–13
opinion copy 90
opinion pages 57, 89–91, 225
opinions 35, 37, 296–7
opportunity to reply 308
orphan 334
outspoken comment 35
overmatter 334

pagination 334
Patel, Roshni 266–7
Paxman, Jeremy 161

payment for articles 85, 312–13
perfect bound 334
personal contact 3, 80–1
personal relationships 143–5, 219–20,
    245–6, 250–1
personal visits 129–30
personalities 41–5
Peters, Sally 229
phone-ins 180
photographs 270, 293, 297–9
pims.co.uk 197
Pink, Stephen 230
pitches by PR agencies 256–8
pitching story ideas 130–4
  hooking a journalist's attention
      33–40, 133–4, 294
  use of jargon 132–3
pix 334
point size 334
Politicos 11
postal contact 80, 128
Power, Michael 94
PR professionals 249–67
  agencies 252–60
  in-house PR departments 262
  journalists' view of 250–1, 269
preferred contacts of journalists 224–6,
    275
presenting press releases 292–3
presenting product information 7–8
press audits 202–3, 204
Press Complaints Commission 241,
    242, 307
press conferences 50, 60–7, 147–8, 276
  acceptances and no-shows 62, 63

at trade shows 74
catering and seating arrangements 64
and competition between journalists
    82
dress codes 64
embargoes 66, 270, 299–300, 331
following-up 222
guest list 62, 63
non-disclosure agreements (NDAs)
    66–7
positives and negatives 61
programme 65
rehearsal of speakers 64
timing 62
venues 62
virtual press conferences 208–9
press days 148–9, 334
press enquiries 227–8
press monitoring services 212
press pack 334
press receptions 67–9, 74
  and unforeseen events 147–8
press releases 3, 269–72, 287–304
  content 294–5
  distribution 200–3, 271, 273, 303
  embargoes 270, 299–300
  expert opinion 296–7
  failed press releases 304
  following-up 220–2, 270
  hooking a journalist's attention
      33–40, 133–4, 294
  importance of 287–9
  journalists' response on receipt 300–1
  length of 270–1, 292
  and photographs 270, 293, 297–9

presentation 292–3
  and quotes 295–7
  successful 288–9
  targeting 292
  teaser campaigns 136–7, 271
  writing style 290–2, 301–3
press services 202
Price, John 93
primary research 32
print editors 19–20
print media 12, 13
privacy 308
prnewswire.co.uk 197
producers 19, 334
production editors 20
production frequency 21, 141
products
  life cycles 111–12
  presenting information on 7–8,
    29–30
  reviews 55–6, 93
  SWOT analysis 103–4
  tests and comparisons 55–6
profnet.co.uk 197
protecting sources of information 272,
  311
Public Relations Consultants
  Association 256
publication process 123–4
publishers 19, 334–5
pull quote 335
pundit of choice objective 224–6, 275

qualitative message evaluation 263–4
qualitative research 32

quantitative message evaluation 263
quantitative research 32
questions
  answering 172
  anticipating 108–11
  avoiding 167
  hostile 175–6
  No Comment responses 154, 155, 185
  not to ask 184–6
  rehearsing responses 111
  standard responses 110
quotes 4, 21, 225, 295–7
  pundit of choice objective 224–6, 275

radio 12, 13
  see also television/radio interviews
Ratner, Gerald 2
readers' competitions 59–60, 226
receptions see press receptions
recommended products 55–6
recorded conversations 8–9
red top 335
refusing interviews 153–5
relationships with journalists 143–5,
  219–20, 245–6, 250–1
remote TV studios 180
reporters 335
reputation management 215–16, 238
  brand reputation 233–4
researchers 20–1
Response Source 197
return on investment 263
reviews editors 56
reviews of products 55–6, 93
right of reply 240, 242, 308

Roddick, Anita 41
roles
    of editors 5, 123
    of journalists 4–5
running head 335

sales messages 105
sales talk 273
script 335
Seasoned Professionals 11–12
secondary research 32
selecting agencies 253, 256–8
self-image of journalists 4
seminars 72–3
seniority of contacts 122–5
sex cases 310, 311
shop visits 75
show stands 73–5
sic 335
side-head 335
sidebar 335
simplywebcast.com 208
slander 244
slug 336
sound bite 336
Sourcewire 140, 197
spam 336
speaking techniques 177–8
special briefings 83
Specialists 11
spike 336
spokespeople 30
sponsored pages 226
staff journalists 14–15, 120, 123, 274
standfirst 336

starting an interviews 168
statistics and facts 34–5, 100–5
stereotypes of journalists 6
stet 336
stories 336
    background information 37
    controversial views 9, 35–6
    exclusive stories 134, 331
    facts and statistics 34–5, 100–5
    feature stories 17–18, 34
    headlines 34, 332
    hooking a journalist's attention
        33–40, 133–4, 294
    identifying stories 29–30
    keeping stories alive 226–7
    news stories 17, 34
    opinions 35, 37, 296–7
    pitching story ideas 130–4
    points of difference 37–8
    publication process 123–4
    relevance to the readership 36–7
    timing 39
    see also message development
strapline 336
stunts 136–7, 277
style sheet 336–7
sub-editors 20, 124, 216–17, 337
surveys 32
SWOT analysis 103–4

tabloids 337
tape recorders 8–9
target audiences 5, 28–31, 36–7, 292
Taylor, Ellen 266
teaser campaigns 136–7, 271

telephone contact 80, 127
telephone interviews 51, 57, 158, 160, 169
telephone surveys 32
television/radio interviews 12, 13–14, 176–80
  body language 178
  dress code 179
  Green Room hospitality 176
  mobile broadcasts 179–80
  phone-ins 180
  remote TV studios 180
  speaking techniques 177–8
  see also interviews
Terriers 10
testimonials 105
tests and comparisons of products 55–6
text 337
thanking journalists 184–5, 224, 275
timing stories 39
Tomorrow, Alice 216–17
trade names 338
trade shows 74
training see media training
trips 78–9, 275
trusting journalists 4, 181–3
typo 338

URL (Uniform Resource Locator) 338

videoconferencing 198
virtual press conferences 208–9
voice-over-internet (VoIP) technology 198
voicemail 128–9

WAP (wireless application protocol) 209
Wasters 11
web offset 338
web sites 81, 279–84
  company 205–8
  forums 210
  journalists' 209–10
  media service 196–8
  news 210–12
  see also computer-aided journalism; internet
web-casting 208
weekly publications, deadlines 141
weighted effectiveness measurements 262
White, Sam 148–9
widow 338
Winos 11
WOB (white on black) 338
work experience students 229
work patterns of journalists 8–9, 267
workshops 72–3
writing messages 99–100
writing press releases 290–2, 301–3